AWAKE

AMERICA'S FINAL
GREAT AWAKENING

TIM THOMPSON

DEDICATION

I would like to dedicate this book to my earthly father, who instilled in me at a very early age the importance of eagerly awaiting the imminent Day of the Lord. For that, I am eternally grateful.

CONTENTS

FOREWORD
BY DON STEWART

To say we live in "perilous times" is an understatement. People everywhere are looking here and there for answers—for solutions—to help them understand the times in which they are living.

Fortunately, there are answers, and they're only found in one place—the Bible.

I'm so glad my friend Tim Thompson has written this book, explaining from a biblical perspective how we got to this place in our world, what's going on right now, and where we go from here.

It's a call for Christians, including Christian leaders, to "live what you believe."

Tim is not merely an armchair spectator. As you will read, he's been on the frontlines during this very difficult time for our country and the world.

Therefore, I give the highest recommendation for this book. Please read it, and tell others to read it also.

INTRODUCTION

As a child, my father instilled in me the expectation of the return of the Lord. He read sections of Scripture to me pertaining to the Tribulation period and taught me about the Rapture and how it could happen at any minute. Even though he believed we could be called up to be with the Lord at any moment and was spiritually prepared for that to take place, he lived as though it would never happen in his lifetime. Also, he raised me with a tremendous amount of love. To this day, he loves my mother. He loves my siblings. He loves the Lord and His Bride, the Church. I am eternally grateful for my upbringing.

As I grew into adulthood and raised a family of my own, I endeavored to impart the same values and beliefs.

I've told them over the years, "We need to occupy ourselves until Jesus returns! I don't know when He's coming back. But I know He is. And when He does, I want to be found busy!"

That same attitude influenced my work ethic, and as I found myself in full-time ministry, I—like other pastors— spent a lot of time trying to *be busy* for the Lord. I don't know when it happened, but in all of the busyness, I found myself asleep to the Body of Christ. I don't mean I was asleep spiritually. I had my own personal trials. I sought the Lord's strength, wisdom, and leading to get through them. As a pastor, I even helped others address their own personal trials and tribulations. I prayed with them and gave counsel from God's Word. So when I say I was asleep to the Body of Christ, what I mean is the Church as a whole was not cognizant of how connected we are or the spiritual war being waged against it.

God had to wake me up, and He used a few key circumstances in my life to challenge me and open my eyes to what was happening to the Church. Several years ago, I

4

was asked to take a trip to Washington, D.C., and I wasn't particularly enthusiastic about going just to sit through meetings and hear a bunch of "political stuff," but as a person who loves America and has a great appreciation for our founding, touring the nation's capital did sound appealing.

Why D.C., though? I'm a pastor. Pastors don't get involved in politics. We just preach the Word. That was my attitude. I knew prophecy. I had a heart for it, but I had yet to realize I couldn't be a teacher of God's Word and ignore the political issues our culture faced. Going to D.C. opened my eyes to that reality and fundamentally changed my life.

When I arrived in D.C., I attended a series of conferences and meetings. One of those was with a man named Ken Calvert. To be honest, I had no clue who he was. I walked into his office, sat down in a chair across the desk from him, and he asked me, "What questions do you have for me?" I wanted to say, "I don't know. I don't even know who you are!" I quickly tried to think up a question that wouldn't make me sound like an idiot. What made the situation even more awkward was that Ken Calvert was *Congressman* Ken Calvert of California's Forty-second Congressional District—my district. I was sitting across the desk from the man who represented me, my family, my congregation, and my community in the House, and I had zero clue who he was. That's a problem.

You've heard pastors preach about Paul in 1 Timothy 2:1-2 (New King James Version) when he instructs Timothy, saying, "I exhort first of all that supplications, prayers, intercessions, and giving of thanks be made for all men, *for kings and all who are in authority*, that we may lead a quiet and peaceable life in all godliness and reverence" (emphasis added).

These instructions were given so aspiring young pastors would know how to act and carry out their ministry. Pastors have even said, "Okay, the Lord tells us to pray for all those who are in authority, so let's pray right now." Then they go on to pray something like this: "Lord, we pray for our president. Give him wisdom, and help him to lead us well." That's so generic it could make you vomit.

If you ask most spiritual leaders if they've ever taught that verse, most will likely say yes. We *should* be asking them to tell us who is on the local school board, city council, county board of supervisors, state senate, and state assembly. I guarantee you most pastors haven't a clue who any of those people are unless one of them happens to go to their church.

How do I pray for somebody I don't even know? And if I do know who they are, but I don't talk with them and ask them how I can be praying for them, how am I rightly doing what God's called me to do as a pastor? The answer is, I'm not. And that's embarrassing for me to say, but it's the truth. God had to confront me with that.

When I returned home, I set out to conduct a course correction for my ministry. I arranged a meeting with the mayor of my city. That time, I sat across the desk from an elected official with a purpose. I wanted to know who he was, what his struggles were, and how I could pray for him and partner with him in the community. But it was an awkward conversation. He kept trying to steer it toward answering what he seemed to think was the obvious question. "What did I want *from* him?" He appeared bewildered that I just wanted to begin a relationship so I knew how to pray for him. When I asked him how many times a pastor had met with him, sadly, his response was, "This is a first."

This personal awakening also affected my preaching. I quickly realized the radical left had politicized every biblical and moral issue—borders, race, sexuality, gender, marriage, life, and family. Because God's Word has much to say about these things, I realized I should too. How could I say I just preach the Word and not address these issues? So I began to include these topics in my preaching, coupling them with what the Lord told us to expect around the time of His return, and they became so prevalent it scared some people away. I even had a church split because of accusations I wasn't good at preaching because the messages were making the congregation shrink in size. In hindsight, I understand God was removing the people around me who would have hindered me from taking the stances God wanted me to take. That season of pruning was one of the most challenging times of ministry for my wife and me, but God was exercising us for what would lie ahead.

In the spring of 2020, God began what I call America's Fifth and Final Great Awakening. Part and parcel to God's character, He used for good that which the enemy meant for evil. The COVID-19 virus, a very real and serious issue, swept through our nation. How it got here and who sent it is not debated in this book. What I will outline for you, however, is how this situation has been used to attack the Church in a way we have never seen before in our lifetime.

Ignoring the First Amendment, the state of California ordered churches to shut down, and pastors capitulated. For several reasons, many of which I will share with you, I did not. Because of my stance, I was invited to speak on behalf of churches at a peaceful protest in Sacramento, California.

On May 1, 2020, I stood at the west steps of the California State Capitol and preached a message from the books of Hebrews and Romans to explain my position. The event was amazing! Approximately ten thousand people attended. Peaceful, freedom-loving Americans from all walks of life were there. It was like a fourth of July celebration without the beer and steaks. People were dressed in red, white, and blue, and some even wore American flags as capes. The California Highway Patrol was there on foot and on bicycles, and many officers were not wearing masks or social distancing. They were mixed in with the crowd, and they appeared to be having a great time until they were ordered to put on riot gear and push everyone off the property.

Californians were there in protest of the governor's lockdown mandates, not the California Highway Patrol or any other law enforcement for that matter. Gavin Newsom flipped the narrative. Prior to the riot gear, the mainstream media was nowhere to be found. Once the order was given to disperse the crowd, the media came out of the woodwork, including several news helicopters hovering over us, trying to capture the event. As soon as that began, one officer pointed me out to another, who promptly reached over, grabbed me, pulled me in, and took me into custody.

I was arrested and charged with violating 1861(b) of the Rules Applicable to Use of State Property, which states, "Obstructing or Interfering with the Usual Use of State Property. Said person, alone or in conjunction with others, is obstructing or interfering with the usual use of entrances, foyers, corridors, offices, elevators, stairways, garages, or parking lots, or is creating a health and/or safety hazard in such use within, about, or upon state property."[1]

I was also charged with violating section 120275 of California's Health and Safety Code, which states, "Any person who, after notice, violates, or who, upon the demand of any health officer, refuses or neglects to conform to, any rule, order, or regulation prescribed by the department respecting a quarantine or disinfection of persons, animals, things, or places, is guilty of a misdemeanor."[2] I received

---

1. California Code Register Section 1861(b), https://casetext.com/regulation/california-code-of-regulations/title-13-motor-vehicles/division-2-department-of-the-california-highway-patrol/chapter-11-rules-applicable-to-use-of-state-property/article-3-restrictions-on-use-of-state-buildings-and-grounds/section-1861-prohibited-conduct
2. California Health and Safety Code Section 120275, (1996), https://leginfo.legislature.ca.gov/faces/codes_displayText.xhtml?lawCode=HSC&division=105.&title=&part=1.&chapter=4.&article

these charges because I had failed to maintain six feet of separation between the officers and me.

If I wasn't awake before, I was then! The Lord warned us of times like these. In this book, I will identify many of the signs we were given and argue that because of them, the Church should never have been asleep in the first place. We are without excuse. I'll address what happened to the Church while it was sleeping, what woke it up, and how the Church's awareness of what happened to it is continuing to increase. We'll talk about how the Church *has* responded and why it did so in that manner. We'll also discuss how the Church *should have* responded and why it's not too late. As I endeavor to offer suggestions about how the Church should move forward, we'll talk about overcoming evil with good by speaking truth into the lives of others, challenging "spiritual leaders," and holding government officials accountable, especially the ones who claim to have faith in Jesus.

=

If I'm right, and this *is* America's Final Great

Awakening, the Church will have to develop a new

approach to addressing the cultural issues of our day

because what it's been doing so far isn't working. It is time to

be busy for Christ's return.

1

WHY THE CHURCH SHOULD HAVE BEEN AWAKE

If you're anything like me, you enjoy going on vacation with your family. I love it when we get to the hotel because the rooms usually have incredible window coverings that block out all the light—even the soft glow of the evening. I can curl up in the sheets, shut the lights off, and as long as the bed has a high-quality mattress, I can usually get a great night's sleep. But every once in a while, I find myself waking in the middle of the night if I have to use the bathroom or hear a noise. Inevitably, when I get up, I have that "Where am I?" moment. You know, that moment when you know you're physically awake, but you're not completely aware of your surroundings. But it usually doesn't take long before I have that "Aha!" moment. You know, that moment when you remember where you are, why you're there, and how much longer you have to sleep before the worst sound in the world—the alarm clock— wakes you up for the day. So I get up, find the light switch, turn it on, and become increasingly conscious of my environment. You know, *that* experience.

In many ways, I believe God is reaching out from eternity and shaking the Church, saying, "Wake up! Wake up!" And as we start to open our eyes, there's a moment when the Church is awake, but it's not really *aware* yet. For some members of the Church, that "Aha!" moment takes a while to settle in.

When I was a young husband and father, it would take me a long time to wake up. The kids would be crying in the other room, and by the time our daughter was born, my wife had learned a neat trick to get me out of bed in the mornings. She would go over to my daughter and whisper into her ear, "Call for Daddy." My daughter would continue crying for me until she was finally successful in getting me up. Now that I'm older, I wake up a lot quicker. It's funny how our ability to rise and shine changes over the course of our lifetimes.

Similarly, the Church is waking up, albeit at varying rates. Some of you reading this were awake *prior* to the COVID-19 crisis hitting the world. Some of you woke up at the very beginning. Some of you may even wake up after reading this book. But unfortunately, there are those out there who will remain asleep and ignorant of the spiritual battle being waged all around us. They are wrapped up in a spirit of fear and are one step away from God sending supernatural delusions upon them as they reject the truth of His word.

Yet, some people have become keenly aware of what's going on around us—the wickedness in our culture and the agenda against the Church, against the Bride of Christ, against Judeo-Christian values, and against a biblical worldview. They've realized this agenda has its claws in the upper echelons of our government and is inspired by the spirit of the Antichrist. It's in our public school system. It's in Hollywood and entertainment. It's everywhere—even in the Church! But we are waking up and becoming aware, and

I believe that we, the Church, will be a force to be reckoned with as we do. I really believe that.

That being said, I want to address the fact that the Church should never have been asleep in the first place! We should never have been coasting through life in a hazy version of sleepwalking. I think if we're honest with ourselves, we've all, to some degree or another, been guilty of this at one point or another in our lives, but it's important for us to understand that biblically, there's no excuse for it. And certainly, in 1 Thessalonians 5:4-6 (NKJV), we see a prescription for it. A command to "not sleep" as we live out our Christianity: "But you, brethren, are not in darkness, so that *this Day* should overtake you as a thief. You are all sons of light and sons of the day. We are not of the night nor of darkness. Therefore *let us not sleep*, as others do, but let us *watch* and be sober" (emphasis added).

The Word of God tells us not to sleep. But it's not talking about physical sleep. It's talking about sleeping through our Christian life as we await a very specific day in the future that will have intense ramifications for all people inhabiting the earth, hence why the word "Day" is capitalized. That "Day" is the "Day of the Lord." Jesus has already lived on this planet once during His first Advent, and now, people of the true Christian faith eagerly live our lives with an understanding that our Lord and Savior, Jesus Christ, will soon return.

Unfortunately, for those who don't bend their knee to Him while they have the chance, that "Day" is going to be catastrophic. Jesus is going to deal with a world that rejected His gift of salvation. A gift that cost Him everything. A gift that is free for the taking and will give people the ability to escape the unprecedented wrath that Jesus is going to pour out on earth. As Jesus says in Matthew 24:21 (NKJV), "there will be great tribulation, such as has not been since the beginning of the world until this time, no, nor ever shall be."

Later in this chapter, we will discuss the flood in the days of Noah and the fire and brimstone that consumed Sodom and Gomorrah. If you know those stories, you know some pretty painful things have happened. But there is something else coming, and it will be even more terrible. Yet many people refuse to believe this because they have skewed ideas about who God is. In their ignorance, they often explain that they don't like the God of the Old Testament because He commanded that people get killed and caused the ground to swallow up people who wouldn't do what He wanted. They say things like, "I just can't follow a god like that. I like the God of the New Testament because He is nice, loving, and socialist. You know, He's just more palatable."

I ask these people, "Have you read the New Testament? Because Jesus is coming back, and it won't be on a donkey. He's coming back, and He's going to whoop some heinies." This is why we ought to be awake. We must make sure everyone is watching for His return. But because people have fallen asleep, three vital things aren't happening.

First, when people are asleep, they're not aware of what's going on around them. Perverse things have been happening in and around the Church as it has slept. It has been told it isn't allowed on school campuses and that children aren't allowed to pray at school. Members have been told they're not allowed to speak of their faith in the workplace, discipline their children, or pray at city council meetings, school board meetings, or sporting events. But no one is speaking up to combat what's happening because the changes have occurred little by little, so we haven't noticed.

We've been coasting through life, coasting through Christianity.

Second, when people are asleep, they can't defend themselves. Years ago, my friend Micah fell asleep on my couch. (He lives far away from me now, so Micah, if you're reading this book, there's nothing you can do about it! This story will live on forever in infamy.) So my other buddies and I did what guys do in a situation like that. We decided to pull a prank on him. We placed my daughter's Minnie Mouse ears ever so gently on top of his head. But in true "guy" fashion, we didn't stop there. We convinced one of the ladies to paint his fingernails, and after that, we successfully put makeup on his face. When he finally woke up, you could see the "Aha!" moment was still a bit far away on the horizon. Sure, he knew everyone was in the living room, staring at him with silly grins on our faces. But he had no clue as to why. He just had a puzzled look on his face that said, "What happened? What's going on? Why is everybody looking at me? I don't understand." He didn't know what was all over him. He didn't know the damage that had been done. When Micah lay there in my living room, unaware of the devious plans we were executing, he was powerless. He woke up looking like a little girl, and there was nothing he could have done about it.

And this is what's been happening to the Church. All of Satan's wicked plans for us are happening, and it's seemingly beyond our control. Social advances have been made, and many people see them as important or beneficial. But the harsh reality is the Church's role in the public square has been taken over by radical globalists. The role of the Christian parent has been ridiculed, and laws have been passed to usurp their authority in their children's lives. The sanctity of marriage has been completely corrupted. God's plan for sexuality and gender roles has been wholly rejected. False doctrines have crept into the Church at an alarming rate. People have heaped up preachers who will tell them whatever they want to hear. And sadly, the list goes on and on.

Third, when people are asleep, they don't make sense. Have you ever heard somebody talking in their sleep? Sure, words are coming out of their mouth, but it's just gibberish. They truly have nothing relevant to contribute to a real conversation. This is the Church when we are asleep. For every issue we should have a response for, we just spout out nonsense. Unaware, in a sleep state, we have nothing of sustenance to add to a discussion, even though we, the Bride of Christ, should have the answers to all of life's issues.

The instructions Jesus gives us are very clear. The Church must be awake, and it must be watching. For what? Jesus provides us with a detailed list of things to look for, leaving us with no excuses for sleeping. But there are also several other reasons why the Church should have been awake all along. I would like to examine just three of them with you.

1. We were warned in the Scriptures, but we were busy in our unbelief.

The disciples of Jesus, anticipating His return, wanted to know what the signs would be. In response to their curiosity, Jesus detailed a list of things to be on the lookout for. You and I are also supposed to pay attention to these because we're disciples of Jesus as well. The Bible tells us, "as the days of Noah *were*, so also will the coming of the Son of Man be. For as in the days before the flood, they were eating and drinking, marrying and giving in marriage, until the day that Noah entered the ark, and did not know until the flood came and took them all away, so also will the coming of the Son of Man be" (Matthew 24:37-39 [NKJV]).

Jesus's return is compared to what happened in the days of Noah when there was a lead-up to an imminent threat to humanity. There was a point in time when the ark was shut, and nobody could do anything about it. The flood came and took everyone away who wasn't secure in the salvation of the ark. Jesus's return will be similar.

The Antediluvians were warned year after year, decade after decade, of the fate that awaited them if they did not believe. They saw the footprint of the ark beginning to form. They saw Noah building something that didn't make sense to anybody on earth except Noah and his family. Noah told them the flood rains were coming, God was going to flood the earth, and they needed to be prepared. And there can be little doubt those sleepy Antediluvians made fun of Noah, saying, "You're ridiculous! There's no need for that ark! It has never rained like that before! You're crazy!" And yet, he continued day after day, week after week, month after month, year after year, decade after decade until finally the door was shut, the rains came, and floodwaters carried everyone away. They had disregarded the signs and warnings, and they went on with life, business as usual, leading them to their deaths.

That's not how God designed prophecy. God writes down events that are going to happen in advance so you and I know what to expect. As a result, we end up living two ways simultaneously. Like my father, we live as though Jesus is never going to come back in our lifetime *and* as though He's returning very soon. In other words, we raise up godly children. We want them to do well. We hope for good godly grandchildren. We prepare for retirement. We pay off our mortgages. We prepare and live our lives as though they will be long and full because the Lord may not return in our lifetime. At the same time, we live as though He will, causing a sense of urgency to swell within the believer—a sense of urgency for two things. First, for our loved ones to share our faith because Jesus *could* come back today. Tomorrow has not been promised to anyone. We need to be prepared right now. Second, for personal holiness, because when He comes back, we don't want Him to find us asleep. We want Him to find us busy and holy. We want Him to find us set apart for God and for His purposes.

Living both ways at the same time is exactly how God determined us to live; this dichotomy ensures we remain awake. Sadly, I've only seen the Church living one way—business as usual, like the Antediluvians—my entire life. They've been cruising along through life with a total lack of regard for the Second Coming of Christ. We're told in Matthew 24:42 (NKJV) to "*Watch* therefore, for you do not know what hour your Lord is coming" (emphasis added). We're also told in Mark 13:35-37 (NKJV) to "*Watch* therefore, for you do not know when the master of the house is coming—in the evening, at midnight, at the crowing of the rooster, or in the morning—lest, coming suddenly, he find you *sleeping*. And what I say to you, I say to all: *Watch*!" (emphasis added).

Jesus is basically saying, "Listen, when I come back, I don't want to find you sleeping. I want to find you awake. I want to find you watching. I want to find you busy. I want to find you active. I don't want to find you unaware of your surroundings. I don't want to find you defenseless." This is important. We're supposed to be salt. Salt stings as it preserves and kills germs. We're supposed to be light. Light exposes the wickedness hiding in the darkness. We're supposed to be actively doing these things, not saying, "Oh, poor defenseless little me. I was told I'm not allowed to talk about Jesus at work." So what? Talk about Him anyway. "Oh, I might lose my job." So what? Lose your job. Jesus lost His life. Think about it. If you firmly believe God is who He says He is, then you know no weapon used against you can succeed. You know there's nothing that can happen to you that He won't give you the strength and resources to get through because He's got you in the palm of His hands, and nothing can take you from Him. Do you believe that or not? Because it's the people who don't believe who say, "Oh, poor me. I was told not to. I was told not to talk about Jesus at work. And not to sing at church. And not to assemble together with other believers in church." You were told not to? Nonsense!

This is America. We can say whatever we want about Jesus wherever and to whomever we want. It's called freedom of speech. It's called the First Amendment. In communist China, the Church has been silenced and forced underground. If we are not careful, we'll be next.

We were told people would creep into the Church and teach perverted things to the members of our congregations. That they would teach your kids these doctrines. That they would try to strip people away and carry them off to be disciples of false gods instead of true disciples of Jesus Christ. In Acts 20:31 (NKJV), after giving that warning, Paul says to "watch, and remember that for three years I did not cease to warn everyone night and day with tears."

But we stopped believing that would happen, and lo and behold, people *have* crept into the Church, teaching all sorts of perverse doctrines. There are churches across America that teach our children that according to God's Word, being gay is okay because God created them that way. They're teaching our children that sexual immorality is not a sin. We were warned to watch for it, yet it's happening all around us. We've stopped believing. We should have been awake for this, but in our unbelief, we found ourselves busy doing other things and living life, business as usual. And now we see the consequences.

2. We were warned through the testimony of righteous men.

Genesis 7:15-16 (NKJV) gives us details about the flood, saying, "And they went into the ark to Noah, two by two, of all flesh in which is the breath of life. So those that entered, male and female of all flesh, went in *as God had commanded him*; and the LORD shut him in" (emphasis added).

Noah believed God. He was a righteous man who submitted to God's will and was busy doing what God had called him to do. So the Lord shut him in, and salvation was sealed for him. The people outside the ark should've seen. They should've been awake and aware and said, "Hey, can I get in on that? I believe because I see your belief. And I see you've been working on this year after year, decade after decade, and you're still working on it. And all of a sudden, there's some rain. I believe!" But the cold hard fact is, they didn't.

We've seen this same thing happen in our own time with a man named Chuck Smith. Many of you reading this know who I'm talking about. Chuck Smith was one of those righteous men who lived a life dedicated to the Lord. His testimony was strong. He lived his life for Jesus, preaching about His imminent return. He lived in the dichotomy as though Christ was coming back that day—because he firmly believed it could happen—and as though it wouldn't happen in his lifetime. And to his deathbed, he said, "I still believe the Lord will come back while I'm alive." Even though he believed in Christ's imminent return, Chuck planted churches, started Calvary Chapel Bible College, set up conference centers, and established a Christian radio station (just to name a few things). There are over eighteen hundred Calvary Chapels across our nation because Chuck Smith firmly believed in the expository teaching of God's Word as a necessary element of the Christian life. He believed people need to know Christ is coming back soon and that salvation is found in Him. In theory, people shouldn't have fallen asleep because of the powerful testimony of that man.

But they did, and the Bible tells us in 2 Peter 3:3-4 (NKJV) "that scoffers will come in *the last days*, walking according to their own lusts, and saying, 'Where is the promise of His coming? For since the fathers fell asleep, *all things continue* as they were from the beginning of creation'" (emphasis added). In other words, "You've been saying that forever! Oh, the Lord is coming back. Oh, you keep teaching about prophecy. You keep talking about the Lord's return. You keep saying there's going to be the rapture of the Church. Jesus is coming! Okay, okay. People keep saying that, but—it…hasn't…happened!" And they're going to scoff at it. They're going to make fun of it. They're going to look down on people who teach it and continue to talk about it. I'll never forget a man who worked for me years ago at the church I was pastoring. He literally looked me in the eye and almost quoted 2 Peter 3:3-4 verbatim. He said, "You know, Tim, you got to stop talking about this stuff because people keep talking about it, and it hasn't happened. Chuck Smith said those things, and guess what? He's dead." Can you believe that? He even went on to say, "Chuck Smith said these things, and what does he have to show for it? Now he looks like a fool."

Over eighteen hundred churches worldwide. That's a great testimony of trusting in the Lord. Millions of people know the Word of God because of his faithful ministry. And now, he stands in the presence of God, and he's hearing those words we all long to hear: "Well done, good and faithful servant" (Matthew 25:23 [NKJV]).

To me, that sounds pretty darn good. If I could have that kind of testimony for my life after I die, I think that would be pretty respectable. Chuck Smith firmly believed the Word of God, and it was evident in his life. That's how we should be living, even more so now because every day we live is just another day we find ourselves closer to the return of Christ. He is coming back! I firmly believe I will see it in my lifetime. I've been saying I believe we are on the cusp of either (a) the rapture of the Church or (b) the Final Great Awakening here in America. I'll tell you this; there is no option C. Think about it; is there another option? Is there an option where we just go back to sleep? No. We are awake and aware. And should the Lord tarry, we'll be a force to be reckoned with. Either we're going to be raptured, or we're going to let the radical left with their globalist mindset know who we are.

3. The compromises our spiritual leaders made should have woken us up, not put us to sleep.

In Luke 17, in like fashion to His discourse in Matthew 24, Jesus is referring to His return, and He likens it to the times of Lot. He uses two similar yet very different events as sources of wisdom for His disciples: the flood in the days of Noah and the fire and brimstone that consumed Sodom and Gomorra. In Luke's Gospel account, Jesus says, "Likewise as it was also in the days of Lot: They ate, they drank, they bought, they sold, they planted, they built; but on the day that Lot went out of Sodom it rained fire and brimstone from Heaven and destroyed them all. Even so will it be in the day when the Son of Man is revealed" (Luke 17:28-30 [NKJV]).

These two separate situations share a striking resemblance. We've already talked about the days of Noah, but what about the days of Lot when he lived in the region of Sodom and Gomorrah? Ezekiel 16:49-50 (New Living Translation) gives us some great insight into the condition of the culture of Sodom and Gomorrah: "Sodom's sins were *pride, gluttony,* and *laziness,* while the poor and the needy suffered outside her door. She was proud and committed detestable sins, *so I wiped her out,* as you have seen" (emphasis added).

The people in Sodom and Gomorrah in the days of Lot were filled with pride—the root element of all sorts of sin. And just like the days of Lot, our culture is running rampant with pride. As you look around, you'll find we're encouraged to be filled with pride at every turn. Our society tells us things like, "You have the power in you," "You're a good person," "Be self-made," and "You just need more self-esteem." The public school system tells our children these things, and it's baloney! Our children don't need more self-esteem. They need to be spanked on the behind! Don't believe me? Take a trip to Walmart, and you'll see what I'm talking about. Children are so filled with self-esteem it's disgusting. They're all about themselves. Everything in our culture tells us to promote ourselves online to make people think the best of us and to get as many likes as we can on social media. Pride. That's what it's about.

The people in the days of Lot were also gluttonous. This has become a socially acceptable sin I'm embarrassed to admit I deal with. I struggle with my eating habits, as do many others. We're a fat nation. We're a consumerist culture that thrives on excess. At the outbreak of the COVID-19 crisis, Americans took to the grocery stores in droves. Everybody was in line to get as much food for themselves as they could. And don't forget the toilet paper—the item made necessary by a shopping cart full of food and a clear sign of gluttony pervading our lives.

As if pride and gluttony weren't enough, the people of Sodom and Gomorrah were also stricken with laziness, and just like them, many Americans have found themselves living amongst a bunch of lazy people. As the COVID-19 situation continued to progress, I saw hard-working people itching to get back to work. They were seeing the American dream they had worked so hard to achieve slipping away before their very eyes. Unfortunately, they seemed to be the exception to an overwhelming rule. People deemed "essential" (e.g., government employees and anyone tasked with meeting the gluttonous needs of the masses) worked. Meanwhile, nearly everyone else—churches included—took advantage of government handouts, including forgivable PPP loans and massive incentives to enroll in unemployment at an extremely inflated rate. There was such an appeal to the lazy nature of our society that many people even hoped the pandemic would continue because they were making more money on unemployment than going to work. My daughter was with a group of people, and someone actually told her they were making only a few hundred bucks a week at a coffee shop, but because of the pandemic, they were raking in a thousand dollars a week simply by staying home. They literally said, "This is awesome! I hope it just keeps on going!"

In a time of national crisis when people you know are losing their life's savings—people who've built their business for years to pass on to their children's children—and you see their hopes and dreams vanish in just a couple of months, I think it speaks volumes about our culture for somebody to say, "I hope it continues because I'm getting paid for nothing."

We're told the prideful, gluttonous, lazy people in Sodom and Gomorrah also committed detestable sins. If you read the account of Lot in the book of Genesis, one thing you know about those detestable sins is they were sexually immoral in nature. They not only accepted it but embraced it. God says it's going to be the same way when His Son returns. It's important to note that Lot was supposedly the righteous man in his community. He was the man of God. However, his life was filled with compromise. If you read the story, you know he had men in his home, and the men in his community demanded that Lot send the men out of his house so they could have sex with them. Essentially his response was, "No, no, no. Take my two virgin daughters. Here, have them, and do whatever you want with them." That's how willing to compromise the godly man in the city was.

God says it's going to be the same way for us. Remember the people we discussed earlier who say, "Gosh, the God of the Old Testament wiped out all those people because they didn't do what He wanted them to do?" These people will have to face a harsh scriptural reality one day. The God of the New Testament is the same God, and He's going to do the same thing! And just like He gave people a way out in the Old Testament, He's given us a way out as well. In our day, God has given humanity a path to salvation by becoming true believers in His Son Jesus. But instead, the people who are supposed to be godly live in and around sin, saying, "Well, this is just how it is." They haven't initiated change. They haven't stood for righteousness. They haven't demanded holiness in their homes and rejected sin. They've simply assimilated and compromised, which is the opposite of being holy.

Think we haven't succumbed to the same cultural condition as Lot? The Christian community's outcry to my response to a bill passed in September 2020 in California should help shed some light on it for you. For those of you who haven't heard of SB 145, I call it the pro-pedophilia Senate Bill of 2020 because it "would exempt from mandatory registration under the act a person convicted of certain offenses involving minors if the person is not more than 10 years older than the minor and if that offense is the only one requiring the person to register."[3] In other words, if an individual has sex with a minor, he or she is less than ten years older than them, and that is the only offense requiring them to register as a sex offender on the national registry, they aren't required to register. This law allows judges to decide whether or not certain sex offenders have to be listed on the national registry. So these wicked men (and women) can sexually assault our children and suffer little to no consequences. My response to this was simple. "I agree, we don't need to place these people on the sex offenders list so long as we execute them first." We have drifted so far away

_____

3. Senate Bill 145, New York S., (2019), https://www.nysenate.gov/legislation/bills/2021/a416.

from morality, and the Church has been asleep for so long that I've had multiple people who "fly the banner of Christianity" get mad at me for my stance on this matter. This is how far away from standing for righteousness the Church has drifted and how much the Bride of Christ has compromised. We've become complacent to sin. We're used to it. We live in it. It's all around us. It's on the Disney Channel, yet we keep on watching. There are gay pride parades down Main Street in Disneyland, yet we keep taking our children there. There's indoctrination in the public (and even private) schools, yet we keep letting our children attend. Sin is all around us, and our response to it is, "Well, that's just how it is."

For years, I've been telling people about the indoctrination of our children in the public school system. Many people have said to me, "No, that's not happening where we live." I give them hard data showing them unequivocally that it is happening in their district, yet they still compromise. Their children remain enrolled, and they allow the indoctrination to continue to sink its ugly teeth into their innocent, moldable minds.

To combat this, the spiritual leaders in our community should be doing just that! Leading people spiritually. Leading people in godliness. Not compromising in the name of tolerance. The people who should be taking a stand and guiding people toward righteousness have disengaged. And now that the Church has begun to wake up, those who have disengaged will not be taken seriously. Their leadership lacks credibility, much like Lot in the book of Genesis when he goes out and speaks to his sons-in-law. He says, "'Get up, get out of this place; for the LORD will destroy this city!' But to his sons-in-law he seemed to be joking" (Genesis 19:14 [NKJV]). That man, who was supposed to be the righteous man in the city and the follower of God, had destroyed his testimony. He had accepted the immorality around him and compromised to such a degree that when he finally spoke up, no one could take him seriously, and we can't afford to let that happen.

It's not too late for us. We *are* awake. We're becoming increasingly aware of the wickedness around us, and we can stand for righteousness. The doors of the ark are not closed. They're still wide open. Anybody can jump on board so long as they believe in Christ. So let's not live like Lot. Let's not live with this immorality all around us and let people tell us we're not allowed to talk about the solution. The Lord *is* coming back, for sure, and He's going to pour out His wrath! And, as I mentioned earlier, just like in the days of Noah and the days of Lot, there is a way out. The people who believe in their heart and confess with their mouth that Jesus is Lord are not appointed for the wrath that is to come.

We've got the spirit of the living God in us, and we will not be pushed around! Let's face it, the members of the radical left with their globalist agenda are bullies. When I was a kid, you know what happened to bullies? Not what we do today. They received a swift punch to the nose, and guess what? They never bullied anyone again after that.

To be clear, I am not condoning violence in any way. What I'm saying is let's not be pushed around. It took a bigger, stronger person to deal with the bully so the weak people wouldn't get beaten up. Therefore, it's going to take us being the bigger, stronger Christians—the disciples of Jesus who are awake and aware of everything going on around us—to stand up to the bullies for the sake of everyone else. So let's be strong!

2

WHAT HAPPENED TO THE CHURCH WHILE IT WAS SLEEPING

If you have made it this far into the book without putting it down, this chapter will be the true litmus test for you. It's polarizing, and anyone who reads it will either find themselves sharpened spiritually and strengthened with an increased desire for personal holiness and an ignited fire and fervency about their Christianity, or they will put this book down (or in the trash).

It's important for the follower of Christ to take an honest inventory of where the Church is today. Much like my friend in the first chapter who fell asleep on my living room couch, many things have happened to the Church. It was defenseless because it was sleeping right through it, and if we don't fess up to it and wipe the proverbial egg off our faces, we won't be able to move forward in a healthy manner.

Some of the things we'll address in this chapter are embarrassing to admit, and as we move forward to other chapters, we're going to examine what we do about them, how we respond to them, and where we go from here. But this chapter will address what *actually happened*.

In 2 Timothy 3:1-5 (NKJV), we're given a list describing what will characterize people before the Lord returns, and we're told to *"know this*, that in the last days perilous times will come: For men will be lovers of themselves, lovers of money, boasters, proud, blasphemers, disobedient to parents, unthankful, unholy, unloving, unforgiving, slanderers, without self-control, brutal, despisers of good, traitors, headstrong, haughty, lovers of pleasure rather than lovers of God, having a form of godliness but denying its power. And from such people turn away!" (emphasis added).

When the Bible says, "know this," we should respond by saying, "Okay, this is something God expects us to pay attention to and study. This is something we should be well aware of." I think we're all aware the world is in perilous times right now, and the traits listed describe many people. Of course, the Church is supposed to be set apart and different from the rest of the culture, but because of its sleepiness, these same character traits can now be attributed to it. Let's examine how a holy Church could become stricken with such wickedness.

While the Church was sleeping, many in it became lovers of themselves.

As we have discussed, we live in a "me" culture propagated by social media. We want "me" to look good and "me" to have lots of followers and likes. We have filters that make "me" look younger and more attractive. The world ingrains itself in our children from a very young age with the belief that wanting high self-esteem is healthy. And parents are discouraged from instilling in them what God desires us to build in them, which Jesus tells us about.

In Matthew 22:36 (NKJV), Jesus is asked a very important question: "Teacher, which is the *great commandment* in the law?" (emphasis added). In other words, what is the biggest, most important thing we're supposed to do? Every Christian should internalize Jesus's response to this question. He says, "'You shall love the LORD your God with all your heart, with all your soul, and with all your mind.' This is the first and great commandment. And the second is like it: 'You shall love your neighbor as yourself.' On these two commandments hang all the Law and the Prophets" (Matthew 22:37-40 [NKJV]).

Everything that's written about how we're supposed to live our lives hangs on those two things. We're supposed to first love God with everything we are, and our lives should be devoted to knowing and loving the one true God. When we get this right, the natural byproduct will be to love other people. Why? Because we are going to love what God loves, and God loves people. He sent His only Son to live a life none of us could, die a death on a cross none of us would, and be placed in a grave none of us wanted so we wouldn't have to. That's how much God loves people.

While the Church was sleeping, many in it became lovers of money.

Of course, we see this everywhere, but again, the Church is supposed to be holy, separate, set apart, and different from the rest of the world. But because the Church is comprised of people, and because the culture around us has supported us becoming lovers of ourselves and lovers of money, the Church has become much like the world. One prominent example of this is the establishment of "church growth plans" as a major topic of discussion amongst church leaders.

If you Google "church growth plan," you will find 317,000,000 results in less than half a second. That's how prevalent this topic is. Church leaders are searching for strategies to increase the size of their congregations. Why? Because typically, bigger congregations mean more money. However, these growth plans aren't free; you have to pay for them. In many cases, you have to hire a consulting firm. I'm not joking. This is what happened while we were sleeping. Churches have been paying for these plans and hiring consultants to implement programs to bring in more people so they can make more money and so the pastor can wear a ten-thousand-dollar suit, fly in a private jet, and live in a mansion.

It's happening in congregations all over the world. A love for money has pushed church leaders into a perpetual state of implementing these growth plans. Yet God already put together a growth plan. It's in His Word, it's very simple, and it's free. We are told in Acts 2:42 (NKJV) that the Church "continued steadfastly in the apostles' doctrine and fellowship, in the breaking of bread, and in prayers."

They simply continued reading and teaching the Apostles' doctrine, the Word of God. They continued in fellowship, assembling themselves and encouraging each other to love God, love people, and do good things. They continued in the breaking of bread, partaking in communion together. And, of course, they continued to pray together, praying for one another and for the Lord's will to be done.

Now, you might think, "Well, that's not enough. I mean, you've got to do more, right? There are all these strategies we've got to put in place." Actually, a few verses later in Acts 2:47 (NKJV), we're told that *"the Lord added* to the church daily those who were being saved" (emphasis added).

It's God's work to build the Church, not the Church's. We're to share our faith with other people, and the Holy Spirit goes out into the world and brings conviction to people. He draws them in. It's up to us to continue doing the things God has called us to do.

I have the honor and privilege of pastoring 412 Church Murrieta in Murrieta, California. We experienced a tremendous amount of growth as a result of the crisis, and I can tell you honestly, I didn't sit down once with a group of people and consult with them and strategize a growth plan based on a potential pandemic. I didn't hire a church growth consulting firm and say to them, "You know, one day, there may be a pandemic that affects our entire state, and if that happens, I want to know how we can capitalize on it. What could we do to maximize our congregation size?" Instead, do you know what we did at 412 Church in Murrieta? We kept teaching the Word of God, we kept having communion, we kept fellowshipping, and we kept praying together. That's all we did. And guess that? God added to our Church.

Unfortunately, 412 Church Murrieta was one of the few exceptions to a sad rule. What most of the nation saw from church leaders across America was an eagerness to get in line at their banks with an all-too-willing hand extended out to receive PPP loans from an overreaching government. What the nation saw was that the love of money had corrupted the Church.

While the Church was sleeping, many in it became proud blasphemers—unholy, unloving, unforgiving slanderers.

Blasphemy—speaking ill of God or taking the Lord's name in vain—is a violation of the third commandment. When I was a kid, the phrase "Oh my God" had started to become very commonplace in the English language, and uttering it in my parents' home resulted in immediate corporal punishment in the form of Tabasco sauce being poured onto my tongue. Some parents used the "soap in the mouth" trick to "wash our mouths" of such language. For my parents, the burning sensation of hot sauce seemed to be the preferred method. As a young child, it became ingrained in me that using the phrase "Oh my God" was bad and wouldn't be tolerated.

In my early twenties, a show came out called *Friends*, and one of the main characters was a young man named Chandler. His character was notorious for saying, "Oh my God!" Even as I write this, I cringe. The prevalence of that blasphemous phrase increased exponentially as a result of that TV show, and now we've shortened it to "OMG" with a bunch of exclamation points after it. Even pastors have used this on their social media platforms, and worse yet, in the pulpit.

There are programs on TV that throw around the name Jesus Christ—the name given above every name at which "every knee should bow, of those in heaven, and of those on earth, and of those under the earth, and that every tongue should confess that Jesus Christ is Lord, to the glory of God the Father" (Philippians 2:10-11 [NKJV]). And yet, what do many people say when they bash their finger with a hammer or someone does something they don't like? "Jesus Christ!" Blasphemous! And the Church began to do the same thing without even realizing it.

The Church has become unholy and has begun treating holy things as though they're common. For example, it seems the act of tithing at church is all about money and not about the holy moment it is. During the offering, when the bag goes by, an act of worship is taking place. It's at this time in a service when a disciple of Jesus says, "The Lord has blessed me, and I want to give to the Lord." We pass the bag, and collectively, we're bringing an offering of trust to the Lord. It's a holy moment, but I've seen churches pass it with a "hurry up and get it over with" attitude. It's become a financial transaction because everything in our culture rejects the things of God, and the love of self and money has infiltrated the Church.

It's become the same with our time of communion. I've watched pastors walk over to the table containing the communion elements, grab the bread and the cup, hastily pop the bread in their mouths, and wash it down with the fruit of the vine as though they were taking a shot of tequila.

I've even heard a pastor at a large men's gathering drop the F-bomb from the pulpit! I couldn't believe my ears. I looked over at the man I had brought with me from our congregation and asked, "Did he just—" Before I could get the words out, he quickly responded, "Yep!" And then the pastor doubled down and said it again! You could tell he did it because he was trying to be cool and "fit in" with the men, as though using profanity was the method.

I know pastors aren't perfect. Like anyone else, they make mistakes. But I also know the pulpit is holy. What happens *at* and what comes *from* the pulpit matters. It's set apart for God. Pastors need to be reminded they are being scrutinized by God. In the book of James, the Church is told that "not many of you should become teachers in the church, for we who teach will be judged more strictly. Indeed, we all make many mistakes. For if we could control our tongues, we would be perfect and could also control ourselves in every other way" (James 3:1-2 [NLT]).

While the Church was sleeping, many in it became disobedient to parents and unthankful.

As children in the world have become disobedient and unthankful, so have the children within the Church. Laws have been put in place all around us that give privacy rights to our children. The public school system and our healthcare providers enforce these ungodly laws. I'll never forget when my daughter was around eleven years old, and a nurse at our doctor's office wanted to separate her from us to talk to her about her sexual behavior—at eleven years old!

Satan wants to separate you from your child and have these types of conversations with them. And your child will unwittingly develop an attitude that says, "Well, this is a normal conversation, and we have these talks all the time. We talk about it in school, and we talk about it at the doctor's office. It's no big deal." One of the results of these laws having been put in place during a time of the Church's sleepiness is that even churches are doing this now. "Oh, you're thirteen, and you're sexually active? Oh, your parents don't like that? You can talk to us about it. You have the right to privacy. We won't tell your parents. We're the cool church. We're relevant. We're accepting!" It's happening in congregations all around us. "Well, the kid has the right to privacy. I know their parents; they're pretty harsh. They aren't very accepting because they're set in their old ways. They don't understand the modern culture. But we do!"

Our children have developed a sense of entitlement. But they're told that's okay because they deserve the things they have—food, clothing, iPhones, internet access, a roof over their heads, etc. "How dare you, Mom? How dare you not give me my iPhone? How dare you want the passcode to it? I have the right to privacy!" Parents' authority has been completely usurped—especially the fathers'.

While the Church was sleeping, it gave up self-control.

We were warned in God's Word that people in the last days would be without self-control, and now, the Church is the kettle hanging out with the pot.

In 1954, the Johnson Amendment was put in place, which started the Church on the slippery slope of giving away control to an overreaching government. The Johnson Amendment is a provision in the U.S. Tax Code that prohibits churches that are 501(c)(3) nonprofit organizations from engaging in politics. According to the provision, churches are not supposed to endorse or oppose any specific political candidate.[4]

---

4. Exemption from tax on corporations, certain trusts, etc., 26 U.S.C. § 501(c)(3) (1954).
https://uscode.house.gov/view.xhtml?req=(title:26%20section:501%20edition:prelim)%20OR%20(granuleid:USC-prelim-title26-section501)&f=treesort&num=0&edition=prelim.

Weak pastors have cowardly hidden behind the Johnson Amendment to defend their unbiblical position of "not getting involved in politics" because they "just preach the Gospel." They say, "I can't talk about those things because we'll lose our 501(c)(3)." Well, boo-hoo! Who cares? It doesn't mean they can't operate as a church. The only thing that happens if a congregation loses their 501(c)(3) is financial contributions, such as tithing, can't be written off on the donor's tax return. Well, if somebody is tithing to get a tax write off, they're tithing for the wrong reason.

Pastors need to be bold. They need to look right into the camera during their live streams and say, "Pay attention, IRS! If you're listening, come and take it!" I say this all the time, but they've never come after us, and they won't. You know why? The Johnson Amendment is unconstitutional. It goes against our inalienable rights to tell a pastor he's not allowed to engage in the political arena. Nonetheless, pastors have disengaged. They've handed the reins over to people with a globalist perspective inspired by the spirit of the Antichrist. The Church has no more self-control because we've allowed somebody else to take it. We should never have done that. We've allowed an overreaching government to tell us we have to provide abortion services in our healthcare plans to our staff. We have to perform same-sex weddings. We have to disengage from politics. We have to provide gender-neutral restrooms. We've lost control.

During the era of COVID-19, the Church has allowed the government to control when we go to church, who we go to church with, how long we can be there, what we must wear on our faces, how far away from one another we have to be, whether or not we can sing, and how we have communion. This is what's happened to the Church while we were asleep. It put makeup on our face and Minnie Mouse ears on our head, and we didn't even know it.

While the Church was sleeping, many in it became brutal despisers of good.

The brutality in our culture reached levels of absurdity in January 1973 when the Supreme Court issued a decision in the Roe v. Wade case, paving the way for millions of babies to be aborted. When America started allowing the brutal murder of the most defenseless of all human beings in our culture, we were doomed. Unfortunately, it happened to the Church as well.

When a person is able to do or say something about an evil that's taking place, but they don't, that person is just as guilty as the ones doing it. The Church has allowed abortion to continue. It's allowed laws to be put in place such that your daughter can leave her school campus and get an abortion without your knowledge or consent, and she has the right to do so, according to the law in multiple states. I share this information with parents all the time, but other pastors won't talk about it from the pulpit anymore for fear of offending a woman in their congregation who has had an abortion. "I don't want to make her feel bad." Guess what, pastors? I guarantee you she already feels bad, so don't worry about it. What pastors should concern themselves with is teaching the women (and the men) in their congregations what the Word of God says about this issue. Our congregations have become biblically illiterate, especially about sensitive cultural topics like abortion, because pastors have shied away from addressing them from a biblical perspective. The silence on this issue from the pulpits of America is deafening. It makes the Church complicit in the brutality of our nation and shows the world we don't put a high value on living in a society that's good.

While the Church was sleeping, many in it became lovers of pleasure rather than lovers of God.

When my wife and I stepped out in faith to begin my ministry as a senior pastor, she had a great idea to do breakfast every Sunday morning at church. As much as I enjoy being hospitable and creating times of fellowship, I lovingly told my wife, "Don't do that!" She asked, "Why?" I told her once you start, you have to keep doing it. Of course, she got her way, and thus began the weekly routine of making breakfast for hundreds of people. Now, when I say breakfast, I'm talking eggs, bacon, pancakes, fruit, pastries, juice, and coffee. Every. Single. Week! Everybody loved it until I finally had to say, "Listen, we can't afford it. It's too expensive. We need to stop." We just couldn't keep doing it.

So we reduced it down to coffee and donuts, and what do you think happened? People walked into the fellowship room with bewildered looks on their faces, saying, "Where are my pancakes? Where are my eggs?" We very apologetically told them we weren't doing a full breakfast anymore. "But I want pancakes! I want eggs! Where are they?" And people literally left the church over it because they weren't being pleased.

These issues of pleasure plague congregations across America. "Why isn't the air conditioner on? It's 108 degrees outside. It's too hot in here!" The air conditioner gets turned on, and the others say, "It's too cold in here!"

We live in a culture that wants to be pleased—a culture that loves pleasure but doesn't love God. We've become traitors to God, like a wife who has played the harlot. The Church has prostituted itself out to the gods of this world—the gods of pleasure.

Look at the "worship" lyrics of contemporary Christian music. Worship is supposed to be about God, but many of the lyrics today are self-centered. Instead of worshiping God, we're worshiping ourselves. People have taken a position on song selection that says, "If I don't like the worship music, then I'm going to go somewhere else that pleases me. I want it to be upbeat. I want what's going to feed me, me, me." We have become traitors to God, and we love pleasure rather than Him.

While the Church was sleeping, many in it turned into something that appears godly but denies its power.

The power for the Christian is in the written Word of God, inspired by the Spirit of God. That's where the power and authority to live rightly before the Lord comes from. However, there are people who seem godly, but they deny the authority of God's Word. They outwardly "appear" to be Christian but have no intent on actually doing what God says. I call this "flying the banner of Christianity."

How did this happen to the Church? Might I submit to you that liberal professors made their way into Christian universities and seminaries, and they propagated a false, errant, fallible perspective of God's Word. Those wicked men corrupted young, impressionable, soon-to-be pastors. They indoctrinated them into believing liberal nonsense. Then those soon-to-be pastors graduated and made their way into the pulpits of America, no longer believing in the inerrancy and the infallibility of God's Word.

The acceptance of Universalism has become widespread. Leaders in the Catholic Church, including Pope Francis, are now saying that atheists will get to Heaven. Atheists! You don't even have to believe in God, and you'll end up in Heaven? The absurdity of this is mind-boggling. Because of the acceptance of these types of heresies, people have been adopting an attitude that says, "I'm just going to be spiritual. I'm a spiritual being." I've said this before, and I'll say it again. No, you are not spiritual. You are spiritually dead! There is a part of a person God created to be spiritual. That part of us lies dormant, waiting for God's Holy Spirit to bring life to it and ignite a fire in it!

The "anything goes" attitude of Universalism has contaminated the Bride of Christ. Paul addresses this very thing with the Church at Corinth. In 1 Corinthians 5:1 (NLT), he says, "I can hardly believe the report about the sexual immorality going on *among you*—something that even pagans don't do" (emphasis added).

Paul specifically addresses the Church, not the people outside it. He says, "among you." Paul cannot believe what he is hearing about sexual immorality happening in their congregation. What's worse is Paul sees their attitude toward it. He rightly calls them out on it. In 1 Corinthians 5:2 (NLT), he says, "You are so *proud of yourselves*, but you should be mourning in sorrow and shame" (emphasis added).

Paul conveys that the members of the Church had ignored the counsel of God's Word. They had let the culture dictate morality to them. They were no different than the world around them. And they were proud of it! "Look how accepting we are."

Paul tells them they should be ashamed of themselves. They should mourn over the sin that is amongst them. Keep in mind, this is straight out of the Word of God, not the mind of Pastor Tim Thompson.

This has happened to the Church today, too. Check out the "talk" pages on Facebook. Just go to the one in your area and look through it. At some point, you'll find an increasingly popular question: "I'm looking for an LGBTQ+-friendly church. Anybody know of one?" Watch all the argumentative comments that follow. But they're not arguing over whether this is scripturally accurate; they're arguing over which one of their congregations is the *most accepting*. They fight over it, saying things like:

"My church is the most accepting!"

"No, it's my church that's the most accepting!"

"No, our youth leader is gay, so we're the most accepting!"

"Well, our children's ministry leader teaches them that God made them gay, so we're the most accepting!"

When I tell people my thoughts on this topic, they often say, "That's so judgmental, though, Pastor Tim!" But this is what has happened as the Church has been asleep. We've allowed the philosophy of this world to enter the Church—a philosophy that says, "Don't judge anyone!" Christians talk to other Christians and start their conversations by saying, "I don't mean to be judgmental, but…" What do we mean we're not trying to be judgmental? We should be judging the heck out of each other. You know what that's called? Accountability. Years ago, there were things called accountability groups, and there was definitely some judging going on. And rightfully so. Men would tell me, "This thing in your life (premarital sex, drugs, etc.), cut it out. It doesn't belong there. You're a Christian, and you should rid yourself of it."

I would say, "Oh, I feel judged."

And they would respond with, "Good! That's how you're supposed to feel!"

But still, many Christians adhere to the philosophy of this world that tells us not to judge. The problem is that way of thinking is not biblical. Paul says, "When I wrote to you before, I told you not to associate with people who indulge in sexual sin. But I wasn't talking about unbelievers who indulge in sexual sin, or are greedy, or cheat people, or worship idols. You would have to leave this world to avoid people like that" (1 Corinthians 5:9-10 [NLT]).

Paul explains he isn't talking about people *outside* the Church who have fallen into sexual immorality. And I love that he adds in people who are greedy, cheat people, and worship idols. In other words, it's not just sexual sin; it's sin. Period.

We can't get away from those people outside the Church. He even says we would need to find ourselves somewhere other than earth to accomplish that. In 1

Corinthians 5:11 (NLT), Paul continues clarifying this point for the Church by saying, "I meant that you are not to associate with anyone who *claims to be a believer* yet indulges in sexual sin, or is greedy, or worships idols, or is abusive, or is a drunkard, or cheats people. Don't even eat with such people" (emphasis added).

The people he is telling the Church to cut ties with are the people who "fly the banner of Christianity." They're the ones who say, "I'm a Christian," but they indulge in sexual sin, or they're greedy, or they worship idols, or they're abusive, or they're drunkards, or they cheat people. We aren't even supposed to share a meal with the person who says, "I'm a Christian, and this is just how God created me. I don't need to change. You just have to accept it." I tell everyone who comes to my church or watches us online that God loves them and accepts them just as they are. I say it, and I mean it. I say it because it's true. But it's also true that God will never leave a person the way He finds them. We don't have to fix ourselves to come to Him, but he fixes us when we come to Him. There *are* things about us that need to change. Everybody has been created by God, but because of the fall of mankind into sin, each of us is born with a sinful nature. What we shouldn't do is try and justify our sinful behavior by saying, "This is how God created me, so oh well. I'm a Christian, though. I'm just going to keep on doing what I want to do."

The Church in America has opened the door to all manner of sin. In the name of tolerance, we've accepted it. We boast of it. We celebrate it. We justify it by saying it's necessary in order to make sinners feel comfortable in the pews so they can hear the Gospel. The fact is, they should feel very uncomfortable. They should feel very out of place. We must hold each other accountable. In 1 Corinthians 5:12-13 (NLT), Paul goes on to say, "It *isn't my responsibility to judge outsiders*, but it *certainly is your responsibility to judge those inside the church* who are sinning. God will judge those on the outside; but as the Scriptures say, 'You must remove the evil person from among you'" (emphasis added).

We must hold each other to a higher standard. The Word of God is the standard. Jesus is the standard. God will judge those outside the Church, and it's our kindness—the kindness of the Lord—that's going to lead them to repentance.

Now that the Church is awake, we need to acknowledge what happened to it while it was sleeping.

Something we can all acknowledge is that the reality of this is heavy. It weighs on us spiritually, and it's a hard pill to swallow because it's embarrassing. If you're anything like me, you don't want people to see your faults and failures. I think the Church can be like that. For decades now, we've swept things under the rug. We've tried to conceal the pedophiliac behaviors of many leaders in the Church. We've played the ostrich in the sand for far too long.

The good news for us is we're no longer asleep! Yes, these things have happened, but the sleeping giant has awakened, and we're finding ourselves in an ever-increasing state of awareness. So my encouragement to you is *be holy*, even if people scoff and say, "You think you're so holy!"

Yes, I do.

"You think you're holier than me, don't you?"

Probably! What's wrong with that? What's wrong with it is our culture has cultivated hearts and minds that have no value for personal holiness. To be holy simply means to be set apart for God and His purposes, and our lives should become more holy as time goes by. As we're told in 1 Peter 1:15-16 (NKJV), "as He who called you is holy, you also be holy in all your conduct, because it is written, 'Be holy, for I am holy.'"

Once we've acknowledged what happened while the Church was asleep, we are free to be holy because God told us to be. He commands it! Never shy away from that. Embrace it. Celebrate it. Get out into the world with your holiness, and let it shine before people so they glorify your Father in Heaven!

3

WHAT WOKE UP THE CHURCH

What is it that woke up the Church? In a word: oppression. In order to fully understand how and why God used oppression to wake up the Church, we first need to understand some basic U.S. history. This will help shed some light on the cyclical nature of humanity, which I will discuss later in this chapter.

There have been four Great Awakenings in America. Some argue there have only been three because they discount the "Jesus Movement" of the 1960s and 1970s. I would argue that the "Jesus Movement" was indeed a Great

Awakening, but before we get into that, let me walk you through the first three.

The First Great Awakening in America took place in the 1730s. There were a lot of fiery preachers during that time. One was a man named Jonathan Edwards who is well known for his passionate sermons. The most famous one is probably "Sinners in the Hands of an Angry God."

If you haven't read it, I encourage you to do so. He wrote it during an incredible time in America when people were struggling, and the Church was allowing sin to run rampant. Because of that, people like Jonathan Edwards began preaching about the reality of Hell and the people's need for repentance. His message resonated with various groups, including the poor and women who didn't have equal rights at the time. Ultimately, this First Great Awakening helped lead America to the Revolutionary War, and as a result of the formation of the United States of America, the idea of having a "wall of separation between Church and State" became a staple concept in U.S. politics. The words "separation between Church and State" don't appear in the original U.S. Constitution; it's a principle found in the establishment clause of the First Amendment.

In actuality, those words were first found in a letter written by Thomas Jefferson to the Danbury Baptist Association in 1802.

The Second Great Awakening occurred in the late eighteenth century for about fifty years following the Revolutionary War. During that time, the nation developed, and the effects of the separation of Church and State resulted in the establishment of many nondenominational churches. Churches were popping up everywhere. That time of awakening, like all times of awakening, was marked by repentance and personal revival. The Church was on fire as "evangelical religious fervor swept the country, especially the Northeast and Midwest, and new ideas and beliefs spread via the Erie Canal."[5] New York State was greatly affected by this awakening, having a high concentration of churches involved in the movement. In fact, "This fast-moving wave of spirituality and religious zeal, which converted so many so quickly, prompted observers to refer

---

5. Heidi Ziemer, "The Burned-Over District," *Two Hundred Years on the Erie Canal*, (New York Heritage Digital Collections, September 20, 2019), https://nyheritage.org/exhibits/.

to the Genesee Valley [in New York] as the "Burned-Over District."[6]

During the 1850s, America saw the Third Great Awakening, which would last into the early 1900s. At the time, America was in great trouble. Economically, the nation was struggling. Socially, it was polarized with the North and the South fighting a war over slavery. In such a divided nation, prayer meetings sparked a great revival for people on both sides. There was a Great Awakening in the Church, and people from all walks of life were being saved.

These are the first three virtually uncontested Great Awakenings in America. Of course, there have been robust debates over the fourth one, known as the "Jesus People Movement" of the late 1960s and early 1970s. When analyzed in 1972 by sociologists Ronald Enroth, C. Breckinridge Peters, and Edward E. Erickson, Jr. in their book *The Jesus People: Old Time Religion in the Age of Aquarius*, they concluded "the Jesus People Movement had many similarities to earlier historical revivals, such as its pietistic nature and anti-establishment tone" but was "too recent to

---

6. Ziemer, "The Burned-Over District."

adequately assess whether or not the movement would have the long-range effects of earlier historical revivals."[7] However, in a more recent study conducted in 2002 by Christina Barnes Williams, she makes the argument that the "Jesus Movement" did have lasting impacts and should be considered a historical revival because many of the young people who joined or started churches or ministries during the movement "are still influencing American Protestantism and local communities."[8]

During that time, people were angry. There was much opposition to America's role in the Vietnam War, and "the sexual revolution and significant increase in access to psychedelic drugs" gave rise to "an emerging counterculture that rejected what it viewed as mainstream America."[9] America's youth was blinded by a false understanding of

---

7. Christina Barnes Williams, "The Jesus People Movement and the Awakening of the Late 1960s," (master's thesis, College of William & Mary, 2002), 6, https://dx.doi.org/doi:10.21220/s2-ss4e-cs11.

8. Christina Barnes Williams, "The Jesus People Movement," 64.

9. Andrew MacDonald and Ed Stetzer, "The Lasting Legacy of the Jesus People: How an Unlikely, Countercultural Movement went Mainstream," *Talbot Magazine* (blog), (Biola University, July 17, 2020), https://www.biola.edu/blogs/talbot-magazine/2020/the-lasting-legacy-of-the-jesus-people.

what peace and love were, and many became self-proclaimed hippies. However, a revival emerged "from the midst of this counterculture that would profoundly remake much of American Protestantism,"[10] which came to be known as the Jesus People Movement. And as it gained traction, many in the Church realized they didn't have to "do church" the same way they had always done it. [11]

Suddenly, the hippies who would have never darkened the doors of a church building were attending church. Pastors like Chuck Smith of Calvary Chapel gladly opened up to these misfits. Others, who can easily be described as stuffy regular churchgoers, were resistant to change and were upset at the adjustments they would have to make to accommodate their new visitors. Even the style of music incorporated into worship sessions went through dramatic changes. In 1971, Maranatha! Music was founded, and churches brought stringed instruments and drums into their sanctuaries. Many church congregations today benefit from the fruit of the "Jesus Movement," and a strong

---

10. MacDonald and Stetzer, "The Lasting Legacy."
11. MacDonald and Stetzer, "The Lasting Legacy."

argument can be made that it was indeed the Fourth Great Awakening in America.

These Great Awakenings exemplify the cyclical nature of human behavior that is well defined in the book of Judges. To give a little context, it's important to have at least a cursory understanding of the times leading up to it. The people of God—the Israelites—were enslaved in Egypt. God commanded that the Pharaoh let His people go, but the heart of the Pharaoh was hard. Because of this, God sent plagues upon the people of Egypt. Each was an opportunity for the Pharaoh to free God's people without further hardships. Eventually, the Pharaoh conceded, and Moses led the Israelites away from Egypt. There was the parting of the Red Sea, then God's people crossed on dry land and wandered around in the desert for decades. God provided daily portions of food and water, and their ability to be sustained in the desert for such a period of time was nothing short of miraculous.

As the people wandered, Moses went up on Mount Sinai and received the Law. In so doing, Moses acquired a guideline for how Israel would exist as a nation ruled under a monarchical form of government with God as their King.

Prior to Moses receiving the Law, someone could steal from the Israelites, covet their wives, covet their belongings, or even murder them, and there was virtually nothing they could do about it. They were slaves. But then the people of Israel were given something they didn't have in Egypt—rights. God-given rights. With these "founding documents" of their nation, they were charged with bringing glory and honor to God as they sought to pursue life, liberty, and happiness. Herein lies the parallel between Ancient Israel and America. Americans have God-given rights as well. America is a nation that has been called to bring glory and honor to God, but like Israel, Americans are a people prone to fall into the cyclical nature of sinful behavior.

In the book of Judges, God tells the Israelites to go into the land of Canaan to take their inheritance and kill everyone who lived there because the Canaanites were given to the worship of false gods—a practice that is detestable to the one true living God.

However, "it came to pass, when Israel was strong, that they put the Canaanites under tribute, but did not completely drive them out" (Judges 1:28 [NKJV]). Instead of killing the Canaanites, the Israelites put them under tribute.

In other words, they enslave the Canaanites and tell them, "We're not going to kill you. You're just going to work for us. You'll be our slaves. You can work this off. We'll let you live, and we get to benefit from you."

They compromised. They weren't supposed to keep them there. They were supposed to wipe them out, and in so doing, they would have done away with the Canaanites' false gods. But because of their compromise, the wicked gods of Canaan remained and infected the people of Israel, which, as we discussed in chapter two, is what happens when we let just a little bit of sin exist.

This brings us to the cyclical nature of sinful behavior that humanity experiences. It's a historical, biblical process by which God wakes up His people, and the first part rests solely on us.

Step 1: We allow sin to become commonplace.

Judges 2:7 (NKJV) says, "So the people served the LORD all the days of Joshua, and all the days of the elders who outlived Joshua, who *had seen all the great works* of the LORD which He had done for Israel" (emphasis added).

God performed incredible acts for the Israelites to bring them to the land of inheritance—sending the plagues upon Egypt, parting the Red Sea, sending manna down from Heaven, and many other supernatural events. However, if you look at Judges 2:10 (NKJV), we're told, "When all that generation had been gathered to their fathers, another generation arose after them *who did not know* the LORD nor the work which He had done for Israel" (emphasis added).

When it says, "had been gathered to their fathers," it means they all physically passed on to the next life. The generation after them grew up not knowing the things of the Lord, not knowing what God did for their own people to free them from slavery and make the nation of Israel a reality. And that's what happens when people allow sin to become commonplace. They forget everything God has done for them.

We've seen the same thing in America. It took a lot to make America what it is. If you go back and read the history of the United States and study the battles that were fought, you'll quickly see how God intervened. America has a miraculous story. America should never have happened and would never have happened were it not for the hand of God.

Sadly, people have forgotten to pass this down to the next generations.

Now, we're seeing the results of a generation that was raised not knowing everything God did for America. In fact, they've been educated in the public school system to believe God had nothing to do with America and that America is bad. They've been taught that the pilgrims were the first terrorists here in America, which shows you how poor an understanding they have about our country's history. The pilgrims didn't kill anybody. They didn't take over anything. This young generation has no clue because they're not taught true American history in the public school system.[12] Because we've let this slip by, we've taken one more step in the cycle of human nature.

As the account continues in the book of Judges, "the children of Israel did evil in the sight of the LORD, and served the Baals; and they forsook the LORD God of their fathers, who had brought them out of the land of Egypt; and they followed other gods from among the gods of the people

---

12. Michael Medved, "What's the Truth About the First Thanksgiving," (Posted November 13, 2017, PragerU, 5:43), https://www.prageru.com/video/whats-the-truth-about-the-first-thanksgiving/.

who were all around them, and they bowed down to them; and they provoked the LORD to anger. They forsook the LORD and served Baal and the Ashtoreths" (Judges 2:11-13 [NKJV]). Likewise, sin is running rampant in our country. Many Americans who profess to be Christians have foolishly denied God as the one true living God, and have bought in to the idea that "all roads lead to Heaven." They no longer fear Him for who He is. Even though all blessings come from God, Americans live their lives believing their prosperity comes from themselves, propagating an environment where the term "self-made" is revered. America has become a nation plagued with addiction to sex, money, and pleasure. The entertainment industry has made its way into our hearts and minds, filling them with pornographic images, and tempting us to fulfill the lusts of our flesh. Massive amounts of people find themselves addicted to illicit or legally prescribed drugs. Socially acceptable sins like gluttony continue to appeal to our sinful nature, leaving America fat, dumb, and happy in the moment but devoid of true peace.

Sin becomes commonplace, and we've let it happen.

Step 2: Oppression sets in.

Take a look at verse 14. It says, "Then the anger of the LORD was hot against Israel. So He delivered them into the hands of plunderers who despoiled them; and He sold them into the hands of their enemies all around, so that they could no longer stand before their enemies. Wherever they went out, the hand of the LORD was against them for calamity, as the LORD had said, and as the LORD had sworn to them. And they were greatly distressed" (Judges 2:14-15 [NKJV]).

The people of Israel, a nation that was supposed to honor God and live their life properly in accordance with the Law of God, had transgressed His commandments. As a result, the Lord removed His hand of blessing and allowed the enemies of His own people to take control and oppress them. He did that because it's the act of a loving father. A loving father doesn't let his children sin and get away with it; he spanks his children when they do something wrong.

What we find in this section of the book of Judges — and we find this multiple times throughout the rest of the Scriptures — is God allowing the enemies of the people to come in and wreak havoc on them. As an analogy, I explain to people that when my son was in junior high, I would tell him, "Son, you've got to stop doing that (whatever it may have been). Jacob, stop! Jacob, I'm warning you! One more time, and you're in trouble!" And I'd give him warnings over and over again. Imagine if what I finally did was go to his school, take a look around campus, recruit the biggest, meanest bully I could find, and tell him, "Hey, come here. See that kid (as I point over to my son). I want you to go give him a beating."

That's what God did. He allowed the enemies of His people to come in and give them a proverbial spiritual spanking. You'll see the same concept over and over again. God actually says to Habakkuk, "Look among the nations and watch— / Be utterly astounded! / For I will work a work in your days / Which you would not believe, though it were told you. / For indeed I am raising up the Chaldeans, / A bitter and hasty nation / Which marches through the breadth of the earth, / To possess dwelling places that are not theirs" (Habakkuk 1:5-6 [NKJV]).

This is what God does. He chastens those whom He loves because He's not concerned with their temporal happiness. He's concerned with their eternal sanctification, their eternal life.

America, and the Church in America, has allowed sin to become commonplace. Because of this, God has allowed our enemies to come in and oppress us. Politicians are writing legislation attempting to force ministries (like Little Sisters of the Poor) and Christian-owned businesses (like Hobby Lobby) to provide contraception coverage in their health care plans.[13] Christian bakers are threatened with lawsuits if they refuse to bake a gay couple a wedding cake due to their Christian beliefs. Jack Phillips, a baker from Colorado, had to fight all the way to the Supreme Court.[14] God's chastening began to ramp up during the Obama administration. That was God bringing judgment on the Church and on a nation that was supposed to bring glory

---

13. Kevin Wallsten and Rachel VanSickle-Ward, "What's next after the Supreme Court's birth control ruling?" The Washington Post, (July 18, 2020), https://www.washingtonpost.com/politics/2020/07/18/whats-next-after-supreme-courts-birth-control-ruling/

14. Lawrence Hurley, "U.S. Supreme Court backs Christian baker who rebuffed gay couple," The Washington Post, (June 4, 2020), https://www.reuters.com/article/us-usa-court-baker/u-s-supreme-court-backs-christian-baker-who-rebuffed-gay-couple-idUSK

and honor to Him. God has been allowing this to happen so the Church would wake from its slumber, and He's not done. We're just beginning to see what happens when God allows our enemies to be the ones in control.

The type of wicked leadership America has in its government brings oppression on its people. Think about it. Do you feel oppressed? I know I do. This is what happens when sin is all around us. God allows the oppression, and the Church in America is feeling it.

So, first sin becomes commonplace, then oppression sets in.

Step 3: God raises up men who will call for repentance.

"Nevertheless, the LORD raised up judges who delivered them out of the hand of those who plundered them. Yet they would not listen to their judges, but they played the harlot with other gods, and bowed down to them. They turned quickly from the way in which their fathers walked, in obeying the commandments of the LORD; they did not do so" (Judges 2:16-17 [NKJV]).

Once the oppression has set in, God sends men to call for repentance and get people back on the right path. In other words, people are walking in one direction—a direction God doesn't want them walking in—so He sends somebody to tell them, "Stop walking in that direction." Some people respond by saying, "Okay, you're right. I'll just turn around. I'll turn back toward God. Back on that straight and narrow path." Unfortunately, there are even more people who just won't do it. This is exactly what Jesus told us would happen. In Matthew 7:13-14 (NKJV), the Lord says, "Enter by the narrow gate; for *wide is* the gate and *broad is* the way that leads to destruction, and there are many who go in by it. Because *narrow is* the gate and *difficult is* the way which leads to life, and there are few who find it" (emphasis added).

The wide, broad path leads to Hell, and many people are on it. They choose the easy way out, even though they've been told what the final destination will be like. We've seen it in the Great Awakenings in America. God raised up men, including Jonathan Edwards, to call His people to repentance, giving that fiery sermon, "Sinners in the Hands of an Angry God." And it's true. We're all sinners in the hands of an angry God. Our sin angers Him. There is a real place called Hell, and we need to repent, or we'll end up there. These are things that America needs to hear, to be reminded of. But sadly, this message is currently absent from America's pulpits.

When Jonathan Edwards began preaching messages of repentance, something very predictable occurred. Other pastors got mad at him. They had well-established congregations, and he was stirring things up. Due to the societal norms of that time, church attendance was fairly regular, even if someone wasn't living properly. People were going every week, and they were giving their tithes and offerings. The Church was somewhat on autopilot, so you can imagine the cries of the pastors. "Jonathan Edwards! Why must you stir things up? Why must you call for repentance? Why must you get the people all fired up like that? Just leave well-enough alone." They had become comfortable in their oppression.

There are also modern-day judges like Jonathan Edwards in America—pastors like Jack Hibbs, Rob McCoy, Mike McClure, and Tom Hughes. There are spiritual leaders with very large platforms like Don Stewart who are blowing the proverbial trumpet. They're the watchman on the wall. They're looking out, and they see the danger coming. They've been telling people the Lord is coming and that they need to pay attention, repent, and do what is right. They've been calling on the pastors to wake up and start teaching the people correctly, and guess what happened? The pastors in well-established churches tell those Jonathan Edwards types of pastors to shut up! This is what happens when good pastors stir the pot.

So, first sin becomes commonplace, then oppression sets in, then God raises up men who will call for repentance—people just need to listen.

Step 4: God delivers His people from their oppression.

When God sends somebody to call His people to repentance, inevitably, some people actually repent. For the sake of the people who have repented, God sends a deliverer. That's how God works. We saw it through the cycle that took place all through the book of Judges, and we've seen it in the cycle of the four Great Awakenings that have taken place in America.

Judges 2:18 (NKJV) says, "when the LORD raised up judges for them, the LORD was with the judge and delivered them out of the hand of their enemies all the days of the judge; for the LORD was moved to pity *by their groaning* because of those who oppressed them and harassed them" (emphasis added).

The Bible tells us the people groan not because they're sick and tired of their sin, but because they don't like being oppressed. As the COVID-19 crisis began in 2020 and the implementation of mask-wearing became widespread, there were people who said, "I don't like that I have to wear a mask. The leaders in our government are telling us we have to wear a mask, and I feel oppressed."

For centuries, mask-wearing has been used as a tool of oppression by the enemy, which is why I will not put one on my face. I just won't do it. This is what we saw as the COVID-19 virus spread across America, and honestly, God was allowing it.

As 2020 drew to a close and the election process started, a large movement began in which people were standing up against the oppressive leadership in their local, state, and federal governments. However, not all of those people were standing against it because they were repenting for their sins and trying to do right by God. Many were standing against it because they just wanted the oppression to stop. They were standing against it because they didn't like people dictating what they could or couldn't do.

But just like the polarization during the Civil War, people on both sides were being saved. I know this because I've seen it. Prideful people who had been sexually immoral, doing drugs, watching pornography, lying, cheating, stealing, drinking, and coveting turned away from their sins and came back to God. America is a polarized nation, but God is still at work. People are waking up!

So, first sin becomes commonplace, then oppression sets in, then God raises up men who will call for repentance, then God delivers His people from their oppression. The Church is beginning to wake up. It's becoming more aware every day of what happened to it in its slumber. But it's still waiting for that deliverance.

Step 5: There's a time of peace.

Notice in Judges 2:18 (NKJV) that "when the LORD raised up judges for them, the LORD was with the judge and delivered them out of the hand of their enemies *all the days of the judge*; for the LORD was moved to pity by their groaning because of those who oppressed them and harassed them" (emphasis added).

While the judge was there, the enemies were no longer free to oppress the people, and there was peace in the land. That's a beautiful, desirable thing. Those times of peace are important and should be celebrated. But again, as I said, there is a cyclical nature to humanity. The Church in America is experiencing a time of oppression, and God is beginning to raise up leaders to call them to repentance. The time of deliverance and peace have yet to be seen.

Step 6: The cycle begins again, but humanity only gets worse.

When people are in a state of sin, God allows wicked people to rule, bringing about oppression. When the people feel the oppression, they get called to repentance. Once they repent, they get delivered from the wicked rulers. When they get delivered, they experience a time of peace. But inevitably, they fall right back into sin and start the process all over again.

If you read the entire book of Judges, you'll see that's exactly what happened, and it's what has taken place in America. From the First Great Awakening to today, Americans have been sinning and have been oppressed because of it. Somebody called them to repentance, and many people did. God delivered them, and there were times of great peace in America that should have been celebrated and enjoyed.

But one thing we've learned from studying this cyclical process is that humanity doesn't get better. What Judges 2:19 (NKJV) tells us is that "it came to pass, when the judge was dead, that they reverted and *behaved more corruptly than their fathers*, by following other gods, to serve them and bow down to them. They did not cease from their own doings nor from their stubborn way" (emphasis added). In other words, when the people begin to sin again, the sin they fall into is worse than the generation before them. As a result, every time this cycle is repeated, humanity, morality, ethics, and the things we value are all getting worse.

Look at America over time. Look at what's happened. As we come closer to the time of the Lord's return, humanity is going to groan in its oppression. It's going to be seeking a savior and think it has found it in the Antichrist.

While Christians around the world wait for the true Savior, Jesus Christ, Americans are experiencing this cycle and are finding themselves in what I've been calling the Fifth and Final Great Awakening, which began in the spring of 2020 when God reached out from eternity to wake up the Church.

But what caused the need for this Great Awakening? What fast-tracked America to the end of the cycle? It's been multiple things, but one of the major catalysts was pastors disengaging from the public square. They made statements like, "I don't preach politics, I just preach Jesus."

All the while, the radical leftists joined in and said, "If they're not going to preach politics, let's politicize every biblical and moral issue there is."

And what did that do? It silenced the Church. The pulpits of America became ineffective, and pastors became the people God had warned us would tickle our ears. They became hipsters, and with their skinny jeans and love for philosophy, psychology, and cold-brew coffee, they gave control of the public square over to would-be communists.

As we saw in awakenings past, there were highly concentrated areas of revival—areas that would lead the way for the rest of the nation, like the "Burned-Over District" in New York. I'll tell you what we're going to see in America's Final Great Awakening—a high concentration of revival in California. I've had people call me from states like Texas, Tennessee, and Georgia asking me, "Do you know anybody in our state who's doing what you guys are doing?" And I don't. They're saying, "We're trying. We're searching it out. All we keep hearing is what the Church in California is doing. It's as though the pastors in California are the only ones fighting this fight!"

In 2020, God raised up certain men to preach the need for repentance. As a result, the Church, along with massive numbers of people in California, have been waking up. We know that as California goes, so goes the nation. Time will show that California was an epicenter for this Awakening. It certainly is one of the most oppressed states in the country. But where the oppression is the greatest, the repentance is going to be the greatest. This is what God does. He doesn't let His people sin and get away with it. Not here on earth, and not in the afterlife. Our sins need to be dealt with.

I do believe this is the Fifth and Final Great Awakening in America. The number five is interesting because it's biblically significant. It's the number that symbolizes the grace of God upon humanity. I believe this Fifth and Final Great Awakening here in America is God's act of grace upon us, and it reminds me of the song, "America the Beautiful" written by Katharine Lee Bates. One verse that rings out loud is:

> O beautiful for spacious skies,
>
> For amber waves of grain.
>
> For purple mountain majesties
>
> Above the fruited plain!
>
> America! America!

God shed His grace on thee,

And crown thy good with brotherhood

From sea to shining sea!

God has shed His grace on America. We live in a generation that has forgotten that. But I believe with this Fifth and Final Great Awakening, He is shedding His grace upon us yet again. He's sending us through the cycle one last time to wake us up so we can all repent and obtain everlasting peace.

4

THE CHURCH'S INCREASING AWARENESS

As the Church wakes up, its awareness is increasing, and it will continue to do so as time goes by. It's a natural part of the process both physically and spiritually. Jesus's disciples experienced this after His death, burial, and resurrection. In Luke's Gospel account, immediately following the resurrection, the disciples of Jesus were in turmoil. They'd been following a man, many of them for over three years, and had partaken in ministry filled with some of the most incredible miracles you can imagine. Some of His disciples actually knew Him His whole life.

As such, the physical aspect of Jesus being tortured to death by crucifixion must have been the worst thing His disciples had ever endured. After the resurrection, Mary Magdalene was the first one at the tomb. She arrived and found it empty, and there stood the resurrected Lord. Once Mary learned what had happened, she ran to get the other disciples. Peter and John came running back, and even though they also found the tomb empty, they didn't get it yet. They didn't understand what was going on even though the Lord had told them over and over it would happen.

It's imperative to understand something physical had taken place. The torture on the cross was an actual event. Jesus's body died and was placed into a grave. At the same time, a very spiritual thing had happened. It was something that was prophesied, and the disciples should have expected it; they should have been aware.

Likewise, the COVID-19 pandemic that began in the spring of 2020 was a very real, very physical event. As time went by, more and more people contracted the virus, and many of them recuperated. However, there were some, mainly those with preexisting medical conditions, who succumbed to their illness. So COVID-19 is the physical event, but simultaneously, there's been a very spiritual thing going on that Christians need to understand and be looking for. They need to become increasingly aware of the spiritual battle they're in, and there are four things we can consider that will help increase awareness.

1. We need to start seeing with spiritual eyes instead of physical eyes.

In Luke 24:13-16 (NKJV), we're told that after the resurrection, two of Jesus's disciples "were traveling that same day to a village called Emmaus, which was seven miles from Jerusalem. And they talked together of all these things which had happened. So it was, while they conversed and reasoned, that Jesus Himself drew near and went with them. But their eyes were *restrained*, so that they did not know Him" (emphasis added).

They didn't realize it was Jesus right there in front of them. The word "restrained" comes from the Greek word "krateo," which conveys the idea of obtaining or grabbing something. Something spiritually took possession of their eyes.[15] It wasn't that they physically couldn't see, but spiritually, they didn't know who they were walking and talking with. They were simply having a candid conversation, talking about all the events that had just taken place.

It wasn't the first time that had happened to one of the Lord's disciples. You may recall the account of Jesus on the sea of Galilee when Peter and some of the other disciples were fishing, and Jesus said, "Hey! You guys catch anything?" They conversed with Jesus for a while before Peter finally realized and declared, "It's the Lord!" But because their eyes were restrained, it had taken time for their spiritual eyes to discern that it was actually Jesus they were speaking with.

Well, Jesus says to them, "What kind of conversation is this that you have with one another as you walk and are sad?" (Luke 24:17 [NKJV]).

Jesus knows the conversation, of course, but He's getting them to understand the time they are in. He wants

---

15. Blue Letter Bible, s.v., "Dictionary and Word Search for krateo (Strong's 2902)," (accessed February 12, 2021), https://www.blbclassic.org/lang/lexicon/lexicon.cfm?Strongs=G2902&t=KJV.

them to look at it with spiritual eyes, not physical ones. It's critical the Church of today understands this. As we look at what's going on in our culture, what would we say if Jesus asked us, "What kind of conversation is this that you are having?" Because we're all having them, aren't we? We're talking about everything that's going on all around us—lockdowns, elections, vaccines, mask mandates, etc.

On the road to Emmaus, Jesus tries to draw out a very candid response from his disciples. In Luke 24:18 (NKJV), "the one whose name was Cleopas answered and said to Him, 'Are You the only stranger in Jerusalem, and have You not known the things which happened there in these days?'"

Unable to believe His question, Cleopas responds by essentially saying, "Don't you know? What rock did you crawl out from under? Are you the only one who doesn't know what's going on?" It would be like entering a store in the middle of the tightest lockdown period of the COVID-19 crisis without a mask on, walking up to a couple of people, and asking, "What's going on? Why is everybody wearing a mask?"

I was actually tempted to do that on several occasions—just walk up to somebody and ask, "Why are you wearing a mask?" Just imagine the response. They would lose their mind, especially if they attended a college or a university in the past few decades and got indoctrinated with a radical leftist ideology. But that's the type of question Jesus is asking His disciples, and their logical response is, "Are you the only one who doesn't know what happened?"

Everybody knew what had happened those prior days in Jerusalem, and, of course, Jesus knew exactly what was going on. He was pulling that candid response out of them in order to open their spiritual eyes. His disciples were sad about something, and rightfully so. The person they loved and followed had been tortured to death. He had suffered. It was a horrible thing that occurred. And when we talk about the things going on around us today, these are also horrible things that are happening, and we are rightly sad, angry, and frustrated.

People who had been saving up their whole life to have some sort of inheritance to leave their kids are seeing their hard work dwindle away. Family businesses that some spent their entire lives developing and were hoping to sell in order to retire can't retire now because the value of their business has diminished too much. These are the things people are focused on right now, and they are physical. Tangible. The problem with that is it's really not how God wants us to live. You and I, according to 2 Corinthians 5:7 (NKJV), are supposed to "walk by faith, not by sight."

When it says walk, it means live. We're supposed to live our lives not by the things we see but by faith. How do we get faith? It's very simple. Romans 10:17 (NKJV) says, "faith comes by hearing, and hearing by the word of God."

In other words, our faith increases the more we hear God's word. And the more we hear, the more we see with "faith eyes" instead of physical eyes. And the more we see, the more we *understand* that everything going on around us was foretold in God's Word.

But notice Jesus's response: "What things?" (Luke 24:19 [NKJV]).

I love this about Jesus. He messed with His friends just like my buddies and I did when Micah fell asleep on the couch. That's what guys do. There's a misconception about the character of Jesus. Many read about Him and have a vision in their mind of who He is. I believe this is largely due to the artists of the Renaissance period. You know, the portrayal of Jesus in their paintings. He's got a halo around His head, and often, He's hovering three feet above the ground. He has milky-white skin and hangs daintily on the cross in an effeminate manner. That's not Jesus! Jesus was a man's man.

In response to Jesus's question in Luke 24:19-20 (NKJV), his disciples say, "The things concerning Jesus of Nazareth, who *was* a Prophet mighty in deed and word before God and all the people, and how the chief priests and our rulers delivered Him to be condemned to death, and crucified Him" (emphasis added).

Notice their use of the past tense. All of their focus is on the physical. They don't realize the spiritual at all.

2. We need to rid ourselves of personal expectations.

In Luke 24:21-24 (NKJV), Jesus's disciples continue, saying, "we *were* hoping that it was He who was going to redeem Israel. Indeed, besides all this, today is the third day since these things happened. Yes, and certain women of our company, who arrived at the tomb early, astonished us. When they did not find His body, they came saying that they had also seen a vision of angels who said He was alive. And certain of those who were with us went to the tomb and found it just as the women had said; but Him they did not see" (emphasis added).

We *were* hoping, but now we're not. He *was* alive, but now He's dead. The use of the past tense here is noteworthy because it provides insight into the personal expectations of the Jewish people of that time. Every Jewish woman in the lineage of David was hoping and praying that she would be the one to give birth to the Messiah because of the Davidic Covenant—the promise God had made in 2 Samuel 7 that the Messiah would come through the line of David and that His throne would be eternal. So the Jewish people in that time were hoping that when He showed up, He would rid them of the Roman rule over them, establish His kingdom there in Jerusalem, and rule the entire world from there. That's what they were waiting for. That's what they were expecting. And guess what? It didn't happen!

It was reasonable for them to have these personal expectations. The Old Testament prophecies told believers that Jesus would come once, that He would suffer, and by His stripes, we would be healed. Then, He would come back. We know this by reading the book of Daniel. Those ten toes mixed of iron and clay in Daniel 2 are the revived Roman Empire.

We're seeing this all around us right now. Global elites rule here on earth, just like the Bible said. It's the revived Roman Empire, and Jesus is going to come and tear it all down! We start to become more aware of this when we rid ourselves of our own personal expectations. I don't know about you, but throughout the entire year of 2020, I had a whole lot of expectations. I fully expected Hillary Clinton to go to jail. I fully expected Hunter Biden to be arrested. I fully expected Donald J. Trump to completely drain the swamp, ridding our government of the pedophiles who have entrenched themselves in positions of power. I expected members of the occult in our government to be purged. I expected those things and many others in 2020, and they didn't happen. When we have our own personal expectations, and they're not being fulfilled, we find ourselves so fixed on them we don't see all the other things

God *is* doing. As we rid ourselves of our personal expectations, God begins to open our eyes.

3. We need to consider the whole counsel of God's word.

We need to start taking in all of God's Word, New Testament and Old Testament alike. In doing so, our personal expectations will dissipate.

Look at Luke 24:25-27 (NKJV), which says, "'O foolish ones, and slow of heart to believe in all that the prophets have spoken! *Ought not the Christ to have suffered these things and to enter into His glory?'* And beginning at Moses and all the Prophets, He expounded to them in all the Scriptures the things concerning Himself" (emphasis added).

Foolish ones! Remember, at that point, Jesus had yet to reveal Himself. They still didn't know it was Him, and I love the way He approached them by calling them fools. Have you ever walked down the road with somebody who doesn't know you and called them a fool? It's a bold thing to do. He's bringing to their memory *all* of what the prophets said, not just the parts they like. And it wasn't only the prophets who said those things. The Prophet of all prophets,

Jesus Himself, said those things. Over and over again, He told His disciples He was going to suffer and die. He's reminding them what the whole counsel of His word actually says.

This is why I like teaching the Bible verse by verse as a general rule. It forces the believer to go through things they don't necessarily enjoy. What happens is people tend to open up the Bible and just pull out the verses they like. "I liked that verse right there. I'm going to throw that on Facebook." They focus on that one verse, and they don't read the one before or the one after. That one just sounded really good, and they don't even know the context of it. They have no clue what it actually means, but they like it.

Then they start going through the rest of the Bible, and they say, "I don't like that. I don't really believe that because that makes me feel guilty," or "That means I have to take my brother into account on that one, so I'm not going to. I'll just tear that one out and throw it away." As a result, they're left with an incomplete understanding of the prophetic timeline. They don't see or comprehend what God is actually doing.

It's a dangerous place for people to be, and a good question for people like that is, "If you can't believe the things in God's Word that you don't like, how can you ever believe the things you do?" That's a logical question they need to answer. Either all of it's true, and God is righteous, or none of it's true, and He's a liar.

It was foretold by the prophets that Jesus would suffer and die. It has also been told that there would be pandemics, that Israel would be under attack, that there would be calls for peace and safety, and I could go on and on. All these things were already told to us, and we're supposed to know them, look for them, and be aware of them when they're happening in front of our very eyes. The question for us is not only if we know these things in God's Word, but if we believe them. Are we considering them at this time?

Continuing in Luke 24:28-31 (NKJV), we see that "they drew near to the village where they were going, and He indicated that He would have gone farther. But they constrained Him, saying, 'Abide with us, for it is toward evening, and the day is far spent.' And He went in to stay with them. Now it came to pass, as He sat at the table with them, that *He took bread, blessed and broke it,* and gave it to them. Then *their eyes were opened and they knew Him; and He vanished from their sight"* (emphasis added).

What is it about this act that opened their eyes? The fact is, we don't know for sure. We can only speculate because the Bible doesn't explicitly say. There was something familiar about it, though. Jesus broke the bread: this was common in the ministry of Jesus. We know He fed thousands of people with bread and fish at least twice. He broke it, blessed it, and distributed it. And, of course, the Last Supper had taken place just a few days prior. There, He took bread, broke it, and gave it to His disciples. So, after being reminded of what the whole of God's counsel actually says, there had to be something in that act that was familiar to them. It must have reminded them of Jesus. Regardless, it opened their eyes. For each and every one of us, there is something that God uses along the path of our life that wakes us up.

What was it that opened *your* eyes? I love asking people this question. I've talked to many people, and everyone's story is different. For some, they were watching something on the news, and as they watched it, God opened their eyes. They found themselves realizing, "I'm being lied to right now" while they were watching certain news outlets. Of course they were being lied to! I could have told them that! For others, it was just something that jumped out at them when they were opening the Bible in their morning devotions. They were having that morning cup of joe, and God showed them. He woke them up. Whatever it may be, God opens our eyes and makes us aware; He reminds us what His counsel actually says. For Jesus's disciples, it was that reminder and the breaking of bread.

But notice it says He vanished from their sight. I don't know if you see it or not, but Jesus was messing with them again, and it's kind of cool! He walked with them, talked with them, called them fools, and reminded them what the prophets had spoken. He showed them that their personal expectations would leave them with a false understanding of their circumstances and that unless they considered the whole counsel of God's Word, they would walk through life with fear and disappointment. And then, all of a sudden, when they realized who He was, He was gone! I can almost hear them now: "Wait! Wait! Come back!"

4. The Church's awareness will increase through mutual confirmations.

After Jesus vanishes, his disciples ask one another, "Did not our heart burn within us while He talked with us on the road, and while He opened the Scriptures to us?" (Luke 24:32 [NKJV]). Then, they start to confirm with one another, essentially saying, "When he was talking to me, it was burning within me, was it burning within you?"

"Yeah! It was burning within me too, but I can't believe I didn't know it was Him! I can't believe I didn't see!"

Mutual confirmations were taking place, and "they rose up that very hour and returned to Jerusalem, and found the eleven and those who were with them gathered together, saying, 'The Lord is risen indeed, and has appeared to Simon!' And they told about the things that had happened on the road, and how He was known to them in the breaking of bread" (Luke 24:33 [NKJV]). They got up that very moment and began the long trek back to Jerusalem. They journeyed seven miles by foot to bring the news to others.

On Father's Day in June 2020, I woke up around 3:00 a.m. This is what God does with me. He wakes me up early in the morning and plants something in my mind, and I just have to pray on it. When He woke me up that night, He simply said, "The masks are demonic." That was it. He didn't tell me anything else. He just planted that thought in my mind and left me to start praying.

Before you read on, you should know I'm not saying that if you wear a mask, you are somehow demonic. I'm not even saying masks themselves are intrinsically evil. I understand there are times when people need to wear them—medical professionals, painters, law enforcement officers dealing with unruly crowds. Try and understand that God was doing something in my heart and my mind to accomplish His will.

That being said, I got up and just started praying. I didn't really know what it was all about, but I did know I didn't like anybody telling me I had to wear a mask. I don't like being told I have to do anything. And I definitely didn't like what was going on with the Church. At that point, my church was already open, and we didn't require masks or social distancing at all. But still, God hadn't completely opened my eyes to the demonic nature of the masks. Over the next couple of days, I started reading and studying, getting more and more information. What I found was very disturbing.

Remember what I said earlier about masks being used as a tool of oppression? Well, there are several methods the occult uses to ritually initiate people, some unwittingly. Four of their methods were being used on the American people: the ritual of mask-wearing, the ritual of washing hands, the ritual of social distancing associated with circles and the number six, and the ritual of social isolation with token gifts.

Members of the occult have long worn masks as part of their rituals. The wearing of masks is a form of alchemy—the conversion of one thing into another. We see this during Halloween. Children put on a mask of their favorite superhero, and voilà, they become that character. The wearing of masks is also a tool of oppression. You and I were created in the image of a loving, all-powerful God. Satan hates this fact and desires to cover that image. Don't believe me? Ask any woman in Saudi Arabia. Masks represent compliance and submission to the leaders of the occult who love making people wear them and love it even more when people comply.

In the occult, hand washing is the ritualistic symbol of rejection. The washing of hands dates all the way back to Pontius Pilate washing his hands of Christ. The person involved, even unwittingly, is symbolically washing away their old way of life and accepting the new way.

Social distancing associated with circles and the number six is a hallmark of the occult. You've seen this in movies or documentaries. They place the person who is being ritually initiated into the occult (or a person being offered as a sacrifice) in the center of a circle. Around that person, they place candles or other people in the form of a circle six feet from the person in the center.

Social isolation with token gifts is another ritual they use to initiate someone. They give the person something so that person doesn't feel so bad about being isolated. In other words, "We're going to quarantine you, but we're going to give you a twelve-hundred-dollar stimulus check, so don't feel so bad about it."

All four of these things were implemented at the onset of the COVID-19 crisis. People were being unwittingly initiated into the occult. In times past, when this has occurred, the people in the occult would end up defending it. They would say things like, "We're all in this together," a phrase that became very popular in TV and social media commercials.

I tell people like this, "I'm in *nothing* with you! Nothing!"

But we only hear this response: "No, no, no. We are. We've got to do this."

It doesn't matter if you explain using rationale, logic, scientific data, or the Word of God Himself. They defend it! And they haven't a clue! They're in.

Now, if it were just me who had heard this from God, I would be nervous. In actuality, I was kind of nervous to tell this to anyone. It sounds weird, especially to a person who's not a believer. Telling a secular person, "Satan's doing it" wouldn't go over very well. So I started sharing my experience with people I trust. The mutual confirmations started pouring in. More and more people were waking up and becoming aware of what was happening.

Now when I see people masked up, I see Satan all over it, which is why I decided I just wouldn't wear one. I'm awake, I'm aware of his devices, and the Church continues to open its eyes in a similar fashion.

5

HOW THE CHURCH RESPONDED, AND WHY IT RESPONDED THAT WAY

Certainly, the COVID-19 crisis that began in the

spring of 2020 warranted a national response. It's a virus,

and like any virus, it's contagious and could cause

unforeseen medical ramifications, including death. In the

beginning, doctors didn't know much about it, so the

government got involved, and a national campaign was

launched to respond—only the response quickly seemed to

turn political, not rational.

With every situation we face in life, there are varying ways to respond. Our flesh has one way. When I say "our flesh," I'm referring to humanity in our carnal state. The problem with this is found in Proverbs 14:12 (NLT): "There is a path before each person that *seems* right, but it ends in *death*" (emphasis added).

Once we've decided what our response will be, we set out, determined to be right. We can't imagine we're wrong, and we don't understand why everyone doesn't think the way we do. We even expect that God understands our position and will line up with us. I've been guilty of this, and if you are honest with yourself, you have as well.

The world has another way. When I say the world, I'm speaking of the world system and all the governments of humankind inspired by the spirit of the Antichrist. The world wants to press us into its mold, which is why we're told in Romans 12:2 (NKJV) to "not be conformed to this world, but be transformed by the renewing of your mind, that you may prove what is that good and acceptable and perfect *will of God*" (emphasis added).

Our will and the will of the world don't matter. They don't create lasting changes for the Kingdom of God. It's by submitting to the will of the Father that truly yields the type of results we long for, even when it means we might suffer in the process. Jesus taught us this in the Garden of Gethsemane.

We've already established that the Lord has used the COVID-19 crisis as a tool to wake up the Church. The questions that need to be answered are: "How did the Church respond?" "Why did it respond that way?" and "Did the Church's response look different than the world's response?" According to 2 Corinthians 6:17 (NKJV), we're told to "Come out from among them / And *be separate*" (emphasis added).

Separate. Holy. Set apart. When the world looks at the Church, it should look drastically different from the rest of the world.

However, the Church as a whole hasn't responded well. I understand that many members of the Body of Christ have. Unfortunately, they were the exception, not the rule. The reason for this can be pinpointed to a very specific cause. The pulpits in America haven't been doing a proper exegesis of the Scriptures. When you don't have a proper interpretation or application of God's Word, you end up doing things that don't line up with God's will.

We're taught in elementary school to ask very important questions: Who? What? Why? Where? When? and How? These are all things you ask while reading to understand what's being said and the author's intended meaning.

In December 2019 and January 2020, the talk of this virus had already begun, but the nation hadn't initiated any lockdowns. Then, by March, "COVID," "coronavirus," "China virus," "CCP virus," and "the 'rona" became household terms. America was then asked to shut down for two weeks to "slow the spread," and government officials demanded that church leaders close their locations if they held more than 250 people in a room. Out of an abundance of caution, many church leaders complied. Within a couple of weeks, the goal post was moved from two weeks to a few months, from 250 people in the room to ten.

Then, state governors began very draconian measures of control, propagating a spirit of fear amongst their citizens. In California, Gavin Newsom came out with a three-phase plan for reopening. Where was the Church in those phases? Phase three! With sporting events and entertainment venues! A few pastors, myself included, said, "You know what? I don't care. We're just going to open up." So on the very first Sunday of May 2020, our church doors were open. No masks or social distancing unless somebody wanted to. My attitude was, "That's fine. If somebody wants to, they can. After all, this is America." We had full children's ministry, full youth ministry, and we sang. We allowed people to choose for themselves how big of a risk they were willing to take.

By July 2020, Gavin Newsom put out a state-wide order, continuing a massive government overreach. The order stated:

> Even with adherence to physical distancing, convening in a congregational setting of multiple different households to practice a personal faith carries a relatively higher risk for widespread transmission of the COVID-19 virus, and may result in increased rates of infection, hospitalization, and death, especially among more vulnerable populations. In particular, activities such as singing and chanting negate the risk-reduction achieved through six feet of physical distancing.
>
> Places of worship must therefore discontinue indoor singing and chanting activities and limit *indoor* attendance to 25% of building capacity or a maximum of 100 attendees, whichever is lower.[16]

---

16. "COVID-19 INDUSTRY GUIDANCE: Places of Worship and Providers of Religious Services and Cultural Ceremonies," California Department of Public Health, (July 29, 2020), https://files.covid19.ca.gov/pdf/guidance-places-of-worship--en.pdf.

On July 5, just days after the order to stop singing at church, our first song was "Sing, Sing, Sing." The congregation loved it! Our second song was "Never Gonna Stop Singing." We knew there was a risk of getting the virus. We never denied it was real. We just didn't care. Nothing was going to stop us from singing to Jesus. To us, it was an acceptable risk.

This is how America has functioned for years. We operate our day-to-day lives weighing out acceptable risk. Every time somebody gets behind the wheel of a car, they're agreeing to a certain acceptable risk. Out on the freeway, you could get in an accident and die. It happens to people every year, yet the roads are filled with drivers and passengers alike. This is how societies, especially free societies, work.

Was I frustrated with Gavin Newsom? Sure. But most of my frustration was with the way other churches were responding.

The Church responded by using the Word of God as pretext to justify submission.

I often say that text without context is pretext, and let me explain why. Pretext is when you use something as a reason to justify your actions, but it's not the real reason. It sounds good, and it may even *appear* good, but in actuality, it doesn't justify the course of action you're about to take.

The pretext we saw used by spiritual leaders across our nation in response to the lockdown orders was that Christians should completely submit to the government when we're told to do something. And they used a very specific section of God's Word to justify that course of action.

Romans 13:1-2 (NKJV) tells us, "Let every soul be subject to the governing authorities. For there is no authority except from God, and the authorities that exist are appointed by God. Therefore whoever resists the authority resists the ordinance of God, and those who resist will bring judgment on themselves."

They didn't ask the who, what, why, where, when, and how. They just took that small section of Scripture and said, "This is what it says, so we have to just comply with everything." Unless one has the context of that verse, they will never understand how to correctly apply it. Pastors needed to take into consideration when those verses were written. If they had done a very small review of history, they would have seen *when* it was written and *what* was happening *where* it was taking place.

This letter was written to the Church at Rome in 57 AD, and it wasn't until 64 AD that Nero began to persecute the Church.[17] So Paul wrote this to a congregation in Rome, governed by an emperor who had yet to persecute the Church.

A few years later, it became illegal to be a Christian. Nero proclaimed Christianity was an enemy of Rome and that Christians were to be put to death. He was so cruel toward Christians that he was said to have put a coat of wax

---

17. "Nero Persecutes the Christians, 64 A.D.," EyeWitness to History, (2000),
http://www.eyewitnesstohistory.com/christians.htm.

on them, tie them to a post, and set fire to them to give light to his garden at night as he entertained his guests. You know how Christians responded to that? They said, "We don't care. Burn us." So he did because they wouldn't submit to the governing authority.

People don't take that into consideration. Paul was giving general principles, drawing from how the people had previously interacted with the government. He was *not* prescribing a Christian doctrine for the Church for every conceivable situation and every different form of government that would eventually rule over Christians. He was saying Christians should submit to the governing authorities as long as those authorities do not demand a Christian violate the commands of God.

When we look at the different types of governments around the world from then until now, we need to determine how we would apply this to America today. We have to ask the question, "Who was ultimately the governing authority in Rome?" The answer? The emperor. Of course, they had other people in the government, but the Roman emperor was the ruling authority. The buck stopped with him. When we consider the type of government we have in America, which is a republic, who is the ultimate governing authority? The people.

America's Declaration of Independence states, "We hold these truths to be self-evident, that all men are created equal, that they are endowed by their Creator with certain unalienable Rights, that among these are Life, Liberty and the pursuit of Happiness. That to secure these rights, Governments are instituted among Men, *deriving their just powers from the consent of the governed*" (emphasis added).

So, American citizens are the ultimate authority. The experiment known as America is the first time in history when the authority was given to the common people over those whom they choose to govern them. This fact creates a very distinct difference in how you would apply Romans 13:1-2 to the Church in America some two thousand years later. It's critical for spiritual leaders and Christians alike to understand that you have to do a proper exegesis of the Scriptures before applying it in such a broad way.

In the letter to the church in Rome, Paul focused on a government that would punish people for wrongdoings so there would be order in society. Contextually, we get this from Romans 13:3-4 (NKJV), which says, "For rulers are not a terror to good works, but to evil. Do you want to be unafraid of the authority? Do what is good, and you will have praise from the same. For he is God's minister to you for good. But if you do evil, be afraid; for he does not bear the sword in vain; for he is God's minister, an avenger to execute wrath on him who practices evil."

Clearly, Paul was talking about a government ensuring its citizens lived in a place where they weren't going to be robbed or murdered. Paul was *not* addressing a government that would demand from its citizens that they disobey God's Word, like the one we have in America today.

Another part of a proper exegesis is taking into consideration other parts of the Scripture. In Hebrews 11:23 (NLT), we're told that "It was by faith that Moses 'parents *hid* him for three months when he was born. They saw that God had given them an unusual child, and *they were not afraid to disobey the king's command"* (emphasis added).

The king's command was to kill the infant male children. Moses's parents were ordered to kill him, but they weren't afraid of breaking the law. They weren't going to submit to that. Why? Because it was an unlawful law. They had a duty to go against that law. Guess where they are? They're in Heaven. And not only that, they're in the "hall of faith" in the book of Hebrews.

And what about Esther? In Esther 4:16 (NKJV), she says, "I will go to the king, *which is against the law*; and if I perish, I perish!" (emphasis added).

That type of unction was missing from the arsenal of these pastors who kept their church doors closed.

What about Shadrach, Meshach, and Abednego? They had no concern for their health as they entered the fiery furnace. What about Daniel? He was told he wasn't allowed to pray to anybody but the king. He didn't care. He went home, opened up his windows so everybody could see him, bowed down toward Jerusalem, and prayed to the God of Israel not once, not twice, but three times that day. Why? Because that's what he had always done. That was his custom. That's what God had told him to do, and no government was going to stop him from doing it.

Daniel did it knowing he'd be thrown into the lion's den, and he was. But guess what? He came out! It's that simple. We don't have to fear anything but God.

Weak, fearful church leaders closed their church doors, masked up, and denied their flocks the human interaction they deserved, all in the name of "submitting to governing authorities."

The Church responded by conforming to the world.

What did the world see when they looked at the Church? Did they see something that looked drastically different from the rest of the world? Unfortunately, no. Businesses were told to shut down. What did the Church do? Shut down. Everyone was told to cover the image of

God by masking up. What did the Church do? It masked up. Small businesses were told to get in line for their Payment Protection Plan (PPP) money. What did the Churches do? They got in the electronic queue at their banks, all too ready to suckle at the government's teat. It's a travesty to look at the Church and see no distinction between it and the rest of the world because that's not how God called the Church to live.

If you look back to when God established the Nation of Israel, He told the men not to trim the edges of the beards. He told the people to dress a certain way, eat certain foods, and abstain from certain foods. When anybody walked into a Jewish village and looked around, they immediately realized things were different, and so were the people. That's how God wanted it, and He still wants that today. When people look at our lives, we should be different. We don't necessarily have to dress differently, but there should be something about us that's unique. Yet when the Church responded to the COVID-19 crisis, the world saw no distinction.

The world has been knee-deep in a spirit of fear. What has the Church done? The same thing. They're filled with fear, even though 2 Timothy 1:7 (NKJV) tells us that "God has not given us a spirit of fear, but of *power* and of *love* and of a *sound mind*" (emphasis added).

A spirit of power. The world has not seen power from the Church. They've seen cowardliness. A spirit of love. Love speaks and operates in the truth. The world hasn't seen love from the Church—at least not the kind of love that speaks truth in the face of adversity. A spirit of a sound mind. The world didn't have a sound mind when it was told to wear masks to stop the spread of a virus, only to see the number of cases continue to climb. It saw people all buying into the same delusion.

That was so clear for those who were awake. When the world looked at the Church, it saw a group of people conforming even though God said to be different, to be completely holy and set apart. Why? Because He Himself is holy. We assimilated even though Paul says in Romans 12:2 (NKJV), "And do not be conformed to this world."

God's Word tells us not to be conformed to the world just nineteen verses before we are told to be subject to the governing authorities. Pastors dismiss that fact and shout from their pulpits, "Just conform. It's for our safety. Conform to the rest of the world!"

You can almost hear God in the background saying, "I don't want you to do that! I actually want you *not* to do what the world's telling you to do. I actually want you to come out and be separate and different from everyone else! Have a little faith!"

He wants us to be different from the world because the world doesn't have the answer to a very important question: "What happens after you die?" They don't know. They don't have the answer.

When you watch the world respond to things like COVID-19, their wisdom says, "Because we don't know what happens after life on earth, we've got to hang on to what we have right here, right now, with everything we've got. We've got to preserve life here on earth at all costs, even if that means shutting down the economy and ruining people's life work." The "here and now" is all they have.

The fact is, the Church has the answer to what happens *after* life here on earth. As Christians, our salvation is found in Jesus, and we're supposed to keep in mind that Colossians 3:1-4 (NLT) says, "Since you have been raised to new life with Christ, set your sights on the realities of heaven, where Christ sits in the place of honor at God's right hand. Think about the things of heaven, not the things of earth. For you died to this life, and your real life is hidden with Christ in God. And when Christ, who is your life, is revealed to the whole world, you will share in all his glory." Yet many people are finding "salvation" in the government's ability to deliver a vaccine, ignoring God's Word.

For example, on December 13, 2020, Americans watched as 184,275 COVID-19 vaccinations were shipped out across the nation. The following day, 390,000 more shipped out and would be available in all fifty states by

December 15. That's nearly 600,000 vaccinations in just two days, and they planned on laying out even more throughout the rest of the week.[18]

So there it was. Salvation had arrived. The world was going to be saved from coronavirus, and who did it? The government. That's how Marxism works. You create a problem, then swoop in with a solution to that problem, and everybody will praise you as their hero. That's not to say COVID-19 isn't real. Of course it is. But it wasn't to be feared the way the governments of this world told us. What they created was an environment where people were waiting for the government to save them. And in December 2020, Americans across the nation had 600,000 vials of government "salvation" coming their way.

18. Madeline Holcombe and Eric Levenson, "Covid-19 vaccine en route to every state as health officials say they hope immunizations begin Monday," *CNN*, (December 13, 2020), https://www.cnn.com/2020/12/13/health/us-coronavirus-sunday/index.html.

The Church responded by ignoring all of the warning signs of the times they're living in.

Paul stressed that the end time is drawing near. He tells them to "do this, knowing the time, that now it is high time to awake out of sleep; for now, our salvation is nearer than when we first believed" (Romans 13:11 [NKJV]). Paul knew the people of two thousand years ago shouldn't have fallen asleep, and here we are some two thousand years later. They thought it was close then. I guarantee you it's closer now.

The governments ruled by men are going to pass away. In Daniel chapter 2, we learn about the rise and the fall of the great empires of man that would span human history—the Babylonians, the Medo-Persians, the Greeks, the Romans, and the revived Roman Empire. We've seen those rise. We've seen them fall. Perhaps we see a new empire in the global elites controlling the governments of the world, also destined to fall.

The Bible says Jesus is going to come back. He's going to be the rock that crushes the feet of the image in Nebuchadnezzar's dream and causes the entire thing to come crumbling down. And the warning signs that these things are going to take place are increasing. Watching them is like driving from San Diego to San Francisco. When you first get on the I-5 Freeway, the sign says five hundred miles to San Francisco. You drive for a little while, and it says 250 miles. Then you're 125 miles away. Then eighty. Then twenty. When you are one mile away from San Francisco, you can see it—the beautiful bay with the Golden Gate Bridge in all its splendor. It's so close you can smell the salt in the air! That's where we're at today in terms of Bible prophecy. The Church has responded by ignoring these signs, even though God put them right in front of our faces. It's time to pay attention!

6

HOW THE CHURCH SHOULD HAVE RESPONDED, AND WHY IT'S NOT TOO LATE

The year 2020 was a time in history when people needed hope. It was a year of uncertainty, and so many of us needed something certain. These are things everyone around the world should be able to find in the Church. After all, the Church has been entrusted with the Gospel of Jesus Christ. The Church is the one living organism that isn't comprised of citizens of the planet but rather citizens of Heaven. It then stands to reason that the Church should respond to life issues, especially ones that affect people on a global scale, in a manner that's drastically different than other institutions. Sadly, as we discussed in the last chapter, the Church's response to the COVID-19 crisis was eerily similar to that of the rest of the world.

How *should* the Church have responded? And is it too late? To answer these questions, I'll tell you the same thing I told my family as I was raising my children. "I'm just going to give you God's Word." I'm going to give you what God says and let that be what drives how we move forward. Then, individually and collectively, we can strategically approach the culture we live in the way God wants us to.

The Church should have responded by recognizing that not everyone has the hope of Heaven.

In Romans 12:3 (NKJV), Paul says to the Church at Rome, "For I say, through the grace given to me, to everyone who is among you, not to think of himself more highly than he ought to think, but to think soberly, as God has dealt to each one a measure of *faith*" (emphasis added).

We're supposed to see ourselves as we are. For Christians, that means having the hope of Heaven. We have this hope because of what Jesus has done for us. God has given us each a measure of faith and in Ephesians 2:8-9 (NKJV) when we're told, "For by grace you have been saved through faith, and that *not of yourselves*; it is the gift of God, not of works, lest anyone should boast" (emphasis added).

In other words, you don't even have the ability in you to have faith in God. The only reason you have faith is because He's the one who has given it to you. There's nothing you've done to earn it. Not everyone has that same hope. It's available to them, but they have to want it, and they have to search for it. The Bible tells us that if a person searches for God, they're going to find Him.

Since not everyone has the hope of Heaven, we need to understand what they're putting their hope in because everyone places hope in something, whether they recognize it or not. As God woke up the Church in 2020, everyone was talking about how to deal with the COVID-19 crisis. As I listened, it became clear to me that people were placing their hope in a lot of things other than God. I narrowed it down to four specific things: government, science, medicine, and people. But each of those things will fail. All man-made governments fail because they're comprised of people, and no matter how dependable a person may be, they're still only human. The only lasting government is a monarchy with God as king, known as the everlasting Kingdom of God.

Many people are putting their hope in science. They need to remember that there was a point in time when science told us the earth was flat. Then it told us it was round. Now there are people saying it's flat again.[19] (Let's be clear, I believe it's round). We can't put too much hope in science, as it seems to be ever-changing.

---

19. "Flat Earth International Conference (USA) 2019," Flat Earth International Conference, http://fe2019.com/.

Most people understand that medicine doesn't always work. As with every treatment or therapy, there are inherent risks and the potential for failure. We're already finding this with the COVID-19 vaccines. Yet at the close of 2020, many people put their hope in the COVID-19 vaccine not knowing if it would work and not considering the possible side effects.

The only thing that doesn't fail is Jesus. He's the only thing we can put our hope in and know for sure it's always going to work. We can look at the Bible and know it has been right for century after century. Everything it predicted has either happened or is unfolding exactly how it said it would.

Unfortunately, as the Church was sleeping, it wasn't giving people that hope, so they put their hope elsewhere. They were flying the banner of Christianity, but their hope was in a vaccine. Their hope was in the next government stimulus check. Their hope was in everything but Jesus.

I said early on I won't wear a mask. I won't cover the image of God, and I won't buy into the ritual of the occult. That has been one aspect of my response. But I had to ask myself, "As I do that, am I bringing them hope? Or am I just bringing them an argument? Am I just bringing them a fight that stands for my freedom as an American?" What *am* I bringing to them? Whatever it is, it needs to bring them the hope of Heaven because not everybody has it.

The Church should have responded by not compartmentalizing their faith.

Not compartmentalizing our faith means we're not just Christians at church on Sunday mornings. We're Christians all the time, twenty-four hours a day, seven days a week, fifty-two weeks a year. Wherever you live, wherever you work, wherever you hang out with your friends, you're a Christian there as well. As Romans 12:4-5 (NKJV) says, "For as we have many members in one body, but all the members do not have the same function, so we, being many, are one body in Christ, and individually members of one another."

On several occasions throughout God's Word, the Church is referred to as a body. The Body of Christ. Every believer on the planet is part of that body, and each of those parts has its own function and its own place. You don't grow an eyeball on your toe. They both have their own function, and the same thing applies to the Body of Christ. Each of *us* has our own function. We all live in varying locations. We have different families and groups of friends. Each of us has our own sphere of influence. Compartmentalizing our Christianity does us no good, and it does no good to those around us. We need to bring our Christianity into the workplace. Some may argue their work doesn't allow them to. Too bad. They need to bring it there anyway. In Matthew's Gospel, Jesus says that "whoever confesses Me before men, him I will also confess before My Father who is in heaven. But whoever denies Me before men, him I will also deny before My Father who is in heaven" (Matthew 10:32-33 [NKJV]).

People tend to compartmentalize it like it's just a Sunday morning thing. But we don't want to stand before the Lord one day and say, "Well, Lord, I wasn't allowed to talk about you at work. They said not to." You're supposed to bring your faith to every aspect of your life. As Romans 12:6-8 (NKJV) says, "Having then gifts *differing* according to the grace that is given to us, *let us use them*: if prophecy, let us prophesy in proportion to our faith; or ministry, let us use it in our ministering; he who teaches, in teaching; he who exhorts, in exhortation; he who gives, with liberality; he who leads, with diligence; he who shows mercy, with cheerfulness" (emphasis added).

We all have our own spiritual gifts—different abilities given to us by God. Let us use them! It doesn't say only use them on Sunday morning when we're all gathered together. Take it with you into every aspect of your life. A good question to answer for yourself is, "How have I been utilizing my spiritual gifts since this Great Awakening began?" I can tell you unequivocally the part of the Church that is still asleep has compartmentalized Christianity. Many of those people haven't utilized their spiritual gifts at all since the beginning of the COVID-19 crisis.

There are many people who have the gift of hospitality, making people feel welcomed and at home. When my congregation decided to stay open during COVID, people walking through the doors of our church building expressed a feeling of being welcomed: wanted, valued, and cared for. It's a spiritual gift that God gives people, and due to church lockdowns, there are people who haven't been exercising that gift. Many members of the Body of Christ who have that gift remained at home on their couches. How inviting is that?

The Church needs to recognize those without hope and bring our Christian faith into the areas of our lives that so desperately need it.

The Church should have responded by loving God and loving people.

In chapter two, we discussed the fact that in the latter days, men will be lovers of themselves and not lovers of God. We laid out what it looks like when you're a lover of yourself, and it isn't pretty. In Romans 12:9 (NKJV), we're told to "Let love be without hypocrisy. Abhor what is evil. Cling to what is good."

Hypocrisy just means you say one thing but do another. We have to understand that whoever owns the definition wins the argument. For the last decade, we've witnessed the radical left own the definition of love. They put out their hashtags and their propaganda machines of what love is. They've gotten so blatant about it that when something is clearly in violation of God's Word, they're calling it love. #lovewins. #loveknowsnogender. #loveknowsnoage. And people are buying into it.

But that's not love at all. If we are going to love properly, we need to abhor what is evil. That means if something is evil, we're going to have a great dislike for it. We're going to be disgusted by it. Now, let me be clear.

God's Word is *not* saying we should hate people who are doing things that are wicked. It's saying we should hate the *thing* that is wicked. But what we've seen is the Church buying into what the world has told us. They've said if you hate things that are evil, then you're the one who's wicked, and you're not loving.

When we look at people who are doing those things, we should feel pity upon them because they are held captive by the enemy to do his will. It's very hypocritical for us to say we love somebody and see something wicked going on in their life and just go, "Well, I love them, so I'm just not going to say anything." That's not love.

If we're going to love God and love people, Romans 12:10-13 (NKJV) says we should "Be kindly affectionate to one another with brotherly love, in honor giving preference to one another; *not lagging in diligence*, fervent in spirit, serving the Lord; *rejoicing in hope*, patient in tribulation, continuing steadfastly in prayer; distributing to the needs of the saints, given to hospitality" (emphasis added).

It's telling us this isn't the time for laziness because there's still work to be done. When people see the Church, we should be busy at work for the Lord. But responding in a godly fashion can be draining, especially when we don't seem to get the results we're looking for.

Oftentimes, the lack of results can discourage Christians because they believe it reflects their success in their efforts for the Lord. But the results don't determine that. I've often told my fellow believers that as followers of Christ, there's a simple way of knowing if we're successful in our efforts for the Lord. We find our success in our obedience. If God tells you to do something, simply do it because you love Him. Don't worry about the result because the results aren't up to you. You can't force somebody to open their eyes. You can't force somebody to wake up spiritually. You can't force somebody to believe in Jesus.

Like I said before, it's not the Church's job to add to itself.

God is the one who has to deal with the results. Not us. You

never know what God's going to do in the long-term. It

might take two years before those people wake up to what

you said. We just have to be obedient to do what God called

us to do and leave the results up to Him. We get to rejoice in

the hope that we have.

Once we've established our love for God, we

endeavor to love people, but some people are easier to love

than others. This is especially realized when we are told to

"Bless those who persecute you; bless and do not curse"

(Romans 12:14 [NKJV]).

There are those who wish to persecute us, to silence

us. The COVID-19 crisis was used, in part, by our enemies to

do just that. Hindsight is 20/20. It's pretty clear there's been a

spiritual element to the pandemic, a spiritual attack on the

Church. It's a sad thing to have witnessed, but a portion of

the persecution came from Churchgoers and Church leaders.

This makes it especially difficult, as we expect it from the

world, but not from the Church itself. God doesn't want us

to have a hateful attitude toward them. Our battle is not with them anyway. Our battle is in the spiritual realm, so we should have an attitude of blessing toward them. And yet, we're at war. It's another one of those weird dichotomies we have to figure out as the Church continues to wake up and respond. How are we going to bless those who persecute us while simultaneously fighting the battle God has called us to fight? Thankfully, God never calls us to do something without giving us the ability to do it.

I'll admit, it can definitely be difficult to do what God calls us to do, especially when the world attacks us for doing it. Take, for instance, Romans 12:15-16 (NKJV), which says, "Rejoice with those who rejoice, and weep with those who weep. Be of the same mind toward one another. Do not set your mind on high things, but associate with the humble. Do not be wise in your own opinion."

I tried to follow this command over the holidays during the pandemic. Toward the end of 2020, as my congregation was gearing up for our Christmas Eve service, we thought it would be a good idea to do an invite video. It occurred to me that a video of me reading a spoof on the famous Christmas poem, "'Twas the Night Before Christmas" to a bunch of kids would be humorous and catch people's attention. I gave the basic idea to my dear friend Simon Cooper, and he ran with it, creating a masterpiece poem for our video that was written with the intent of bringing some laughter into people's hearts. So we set up a day to film, and the kids had a blast! We posted the finished product, and it got tens of thousands of views in just a couple of days. It also got hundreds of comments. Some were great comments from people ready to rejoice with us. Others, not so much. That video drew out some of the most disgusting comments you can imagine. Many centered around the widely reported number of COVID-19-related deaths in the United States, which at the time was being reported as roughly three hundred thousand. They said our gathering together was insensitive to people whose loved ones had died from the virus even though we were obeying God's Word.

When I was six years old, my biological father died in a car wreck. Thankfully, my mother remarried when I was nine. She married an extremely godly man. (The one to whom this book is dedicated.) When I was sixteen years old, do you know what I did? I got a driver's license. I couldn't wait to get it. You know what else I did? I drove on the freeways. I've even driven on the same little stretch of the Pacific Coast Highway where my biological father died.

Was I being inconsiderate because I went out and got on the road? That's the logic they're using. It would be like me telling everybody else, "Because you get your license and go and drive on the freeway, you're not being considerate to me because my father died in a car wreck. All of you need to just stay off the road!" It's a logical fallacy. It doesn't make sense, but they've packaged it up in such a way that people actually believe it. They buy into the, "Yeah, you shouldn't be doing that" type of thinking. The Bible says rejoice with those who rejoice. Americans have rejoiced on December 24 and December 25 year after year, decade after decade, century after century, celebrating the birth of our Lord and Savior. It's an appropriate thing to do, and there's nothing wrong with it. So we did, and it was great!

Loving people don't seek revenge when they're wronged. I know that's easier said than done. But in Romans 12:17-20 (NKJV), we're told to "Repay no one evil for evil. Have regard for good things in the sight of all men. If it is possible, *as much as depends on you*, live peaceably with all men. Beloved, do not avenge yourselves, but rather give place to wrath; for it is written, 'Vengeance is Mine, I will repay, 'says the Lord. Therefore, 'If your enemy is hungry, feed him; / If he is thirsty, give him a drink; / For in so doing you will heap coals of fire on his head'" (emphasis added).

Things don't always depend on you. Some people just won't live at peace with you. As the Church wakes up, we need to respond by loving and trying to live at peace with all men and know how to respond when they make it difficult by persecuting us. The natural response, of course, is to get back at them, seek out vengeance. However, that's not for us. I've found it's best to leave that up to the Lord. He's better at it than we are.

Finally, we are warned to "not be overcome by evil, but overcome evil with good" (Romans 12:21 [NKJV]). So, if the Church responds by recognizing that not everyone has the same hope we have within us, and we take the Gospel message to them by not compartmentalizing our Christianity, we'll find ourselves responding in love—love for God and love for people. Then how do we overcome evil with good? What does that look like practically? How do we interact with the person who simply flies the banner of Christianity? How do we interact with other true believers? How do we interact with the nonbelievers, spiritual leaders, and the government? To do all this, we need to have a well-thought-out, very strategic plan that everyone in the Church, personally and collectively, is on board with. I talk about this in depth in the next three chapters.

But at this point, you may be wondering if it's too late. I want you to do something. Breathe in real deep. Did you do it? Is there breath in your lungs? Yes? Then it's not too late! God's not done with you yet.

7

OVERCOMING EVIL WITH GOOD BY TELLING PEOPLE THE TRUTH

The strategy moving forward is to overcome evil with good. If we want this to be a successful mission, we need to approach some very specific areas of humanity: the people we come in contact with on a day-to-day basis; the spiritual leaders in our community, especially the spiritual leaders at your personal church family; and those in elected positions of our government—most notably, the ones who fly the banner of Christianity.

Let's take the first area—the people we come in contact with on a day-to-day basis. We overcome the evil in our culture by telling them the truth. This has become a novel idea in our day and age, but is essential to living a mature spiritual life. Paul tells the Church at Ephesus "that we should no longer be children, tossed to and fro and carried about with every wind of doctrine, by the trickery of men, in the cunning craftiness of deceitful plotting" (Ephesians 4:14 [NKJV]).

The congregation in Ephesus was like any other young church. They were easily tossed to and fro with new "spiritual things." They easily bought into anything anybody told them. Does this sound at all like the culture we've been living in? People buy into anything. Paul was telling the Church they had to grow up, be a little more discerning, and speak the truth. And he gave a specific way of doing that. In Ephesians 4:15 (NKJV), he says, "but, speaking *the truth in love*, may grow up in all things into Him who is the head— Christ" (emphasis added).

As the process of sanctification takes place in our lives, we continue to become more mature in our faith. We become more and more like Jesus. The more we take on the characteristics of Christ, the more we will speak the truth to people—in love. It might not seem like it on the surface, but speaking the truth to someone is the most loving thing we can do for them.

It reminds me of the '80s when I was in high school. During that time, there was a fad, or should I say, an epidemic of demonic warfare. Anorexia became prevalent. You may remember how fast it infiltrated the American culture. It's still an issue that's very real today, but doesn't seem to be as wide-spread and talked about today as it was in the '80s. It was a wave of deception that altered a person's perception of reality. Someone would look at themselves in the mirror, and they perceived themselves as overweight. They starved themselves in an effort to lose the extra pounds. However, to others, they didn't look like they needed to lose a single one.

When I was a teenager, I talked to my mother about a friend of mine who was suffering from anorexia, and I didn't know what to do. I'll never forget my mother's response: "Tell her the truth." It was that simple.

And so a group of my friends and I got together and approached this young lady and told her the truth in love: "You're not overweight. You don't need to starve yourself. You are beautiful the way God created you. What you're doing is bad for you." We continued sharing the truth with her repeatedly over the course of several weeks, and she ended up changing how she was living her life.

Can you imagine if we'd just said, "You know what? If that's what you see, if you think you're overweight, then you go ahead; just starve yourself. We don't want to make you feel bad. We don't want to make you feel like what you're experiencing isn't real, so we'll just go with it and let you wither away to nothing." That wouldn't be love at all. I think we can all agree on that. Love is speaking the truth, even if it's hard to do and hard to hear.

Fast-forward to September 2016. Assembly Bill No. 1732 was signed into California law by Governor Jerry Brown. The law requires "all single-user toilet facilities in any business establishment, place of public accommodation, or government agency to be identified as *all-gender* toilet facilities" (emphasis added).[20]

A new demonic wave had hit America, and we're still in it. The transgender movement is from Satan himself. A complete rejection of something established at the beginning of time. In the first chapter of the first book of the Bible, in Genesis 1:27 (NKJV), we're told that "God created man in His own image; in the image of God He created him; *male and female* He created them" (emphasis added).

Gender dysphoria, much like anorexia, is a psychological condition in which a person looks at

---

20. Equal Restroom Access Act, Assembly Bill No. 1732, California S., Chapter 818, (2016), https://leginfo.legislature.ca.gov/faces/billTextClient.xhtml?bill_id =201520160AB1732.

themselves in the mirror and perceives something different than reality. This cultural delusion has progressed to such an unbelievable degree that it's not just men thinking they're women and women thinking they're men. The demonic activity has become so prevalent that people are buying into the insane idea that an infinite number of genders exist.[21]

As with confronting the lie of anorexia, the right thing—the appropriate, loving thing to do—is to tell them the truth. "No, dude, you're a man!" Bring that truth to him consistently: "You're a man!"

We're doing that person no good by saying, "Well, I want them to feel comfortable. I don't want to offend them. I just want to make sure everybody feels good. I'm just going to go with it. I'm just going to let them have their bathroom. I'm going to let that man walk into the bathroom where my wife and daughter might be."

---

21. Jack Turban, "What Is Gender Dysphoria?" American Psychiatric Association, (November 2020),
https://www.psychiatry.org/patients-families/gender-dysphoria/what-is-gender-dysphoria.

One pastor from a local church in my area told his usher team if a man walks into the women's restroom at church, the ushers were not to stop him. The pastor didn't want him to feel uncomfortable or offend him. His reasoning? "We want him to come back. We'll just keep giving him the Gospel." That's not helping anyone. It puts the entire congregation at risk. This type of logic doesn't make sense.

Fast-forward to the spring of 2020, and buying into the delusions in an effort to make people feel comfortable continued. Put a mask on and socially distance yourself. Somehow, you're safe even though the number of cases continued to increase despite wearing masks. At the same time the case numbers were rising, many trusted doctors published studies proving masks didn't help and that the materials used to make them may even cause secondary infections, worsening someone's current health condition.[22]

22. Marilyn M. Singleton, America's Frontline Doctors, M.D., https://www.americasfrontlinedoctors.com/wp-content/uploads/2020/09/Masks-Science.pdf.

Withholding this information is the same as withholding the truth from a transgender person or someone suffering from anorexia.

The "law of incrementalism" is a Marxist process widely used to form public policy. Powerful institutions introduce something that heads in the direction of their desired result but isn't quite as disruptive. They let people get upset, but then human nature sets in as they grow accustomed to the wickedness, and the sin becomes commonplace. Once people forget about it, the instigators introduce something new toward reaching their goal, and the process starts over.[23] Each time, the end-game ratchets closer and closer. It has worked so well that I've heard Christians say, "I know the masks don't work, but I'm going to wear it to make sure others are comfortable." We've been conditioned over the course of decades to go along with

---

23. Robert Longley, "What Is Incrementalism in Government? Definition and Examples," ThoughtCo, (October 14, 2020), https://www.thoughtco.com/what-is-incrementalism-in-government-5082043.

something, even if it's not true, just for the sake of making sure people feel good.

In the fourth chapter of John's Gospel, Jesus was traveling from Jerusalem to the Galilee. The most direct path would take Him straight through the region of Samaria. However, Jews in His day did not take that path. They would take the long way around Samaria to get to Galilee.

During the seventy years of Babylonian captivity, the Babylonians had sacked Jerusalem. They took who they considered "the best" people and left the rest. Neighboring nations came in and started occupying the region of Judah, and they intermarried with the remaining Jews. The people of Samaria took on the wicked practices of all the neighboring nations. They threw away most of the texts from the Scriptures and kept only the Torah. They set up a temple and an altar to the Lord at Mount Gerizim, which sounds good, except it was supposed to be at Mount Moriah, which is known as the Temple Mount today. So they were worshiping in the wrong place, in pagan practices, not in adherence to the whole counsel of God's Word. They were, for lack of a better term, half-breeds. So the Jews didn't want anything to do with the Samaritans. A journey anywhere *near* Samaria became a journey *around* Samaria.

But Jesus took the path right through Samaria because there was a person there who He wanted to see, and His disciples hadn't a clue. As they traveled, they ended up at Jacob's Well. His disciples went into town to buy some food. It was then that Jesus found Himself with a Samaritan woman.

We must note it was practically unheard of that a rabbi would be alone with a woman, let alone a *Samaritan* woman. Yet, there He was, and He asked her to give Him a drink from the well. Her response is just as you would expect: "How is it that You, being a Jew, ask a drink from me, a Samaritan woman?" (John 4:9 [NKJV]). Jesus's response, on the other hand, is not what *she'd* expected:

Jesus answered and said to her, "If you knew the gift of God, and who it is who says to you, 'Give Me a drink, 'you would have asked Him, and He would have given you living water."

The woman said to Him, "Sir, You have nothing to draw with, and the well is deep. Where then do You get that living water? Are You greater than our father Jacob, who gave us the well, and drank from it himself, as well as his sons and his livestock?"

Jesus answered and said to her, "Whoever drinks of this water will thirst again, but whoever drinks of the water that I shall give him will never thirst. But the water that I shall give him will become in him a fountain of water springing up into everlasting life." (John 4:10-14 [NKJV])

Now, in verse 15, she says something very interesting: "Sir, give me this water, that I may not thirst, nor come here to draw" (John 4:15 [NKJV]).

She wanted what Jesus had to give to her, but she wanted it without any change on her own. She didn't want to have to work for it. In fact, she saw what Jesus had to offer as a way out of getting water in the first place. But Jesus wasn't going to let her off the hook. Instead, He opened up the door of change, and He did so by speaking the truth to her. He says, "Go, call your husband, and come here." / The woman answered and said, "I have no husband." / Jesus said to her, "You have well said, 'I have no husband, 'for you have had five husbands, and the one whom you now have is not your husband; in that you spoke truly" (John 4:16-18 [NKJV]).

Let's just recount for a moment what's happening here. Jesus is a rabbi. He's alone with a Samaritan woman. He says, "Go get your husband."

She's like, "Well, I don't have one."

He knows she doesn't have one, so He says, "Yeah, you're right. You don't have a husband. You've had five husbands, and the dude you're shacked up with now isn't your husband!"

Don't miss what's happening here. He's speaking the truth to her. He's calling her out on her sin.

If the Church is going to overcome evil with good, we need to be prepared to stop apologizing for speaking the truth.

The radical left has figured something out about us Christians. All they have to do is call us names, and we apologize. They call us a name, and our immediate response is to say, "I'm sorry. Oh, no, you're right. I shouldn't talk about that. I shouldn't say that. I'll just be quiet. Sorry I offended you."

We need to stop apologizing. This whole political correctness garbage is just that—garbage! It's a tool of the leftists, and it utilizes the law of incrementalism. Think about what Jesus did. He showed up and called that woman out. If you do this today, especially if you're a man and you call a woman out like Jesus did, do you know what they will call you? A misogynistic, anti-woman, patriarchal bigot! Simply for simply speaking the truth.

Jesus did it. Why don't we? Is it because it's mean? Was Jesus being mean? No. Remember, the most loving thing you can do is share the truth with somebody. It is an act of great love. But we've changed it so much so that if you tell somebody the truth about the condition they're in, somehow, you hate them. Somehow, if somebody is living a homosexual lifestyle, and you let them know that Jesus has a better plan for them, they've determined that you hate them. "You're homophobic!" Just because you call it what the Bible calls it.

"Well, let's just not say anything. I don't want to hurt their feelings."

Do you think for a moment Jesus would say something like this? No. Jesus would tell them, "Listen, what you're doing is wrong. I have something better for you."

Why don't we do that? "Well, because they'll call us names. I don't want to be called a name." And we apologize for speaking the truth in love. In my years of ministry, I've been called every name in the book: misogynist, bigot, homophobe, xenophobe, racist, and murderer.

Because I kept the Church doors open during the COVID-19 crisis, people wrote to the church saying I'm a murderer. A murderer! I don't care. We remained open. I won't stop the assembling of the brethren just because others call me a name. It shouldn't stop any of us. In Matthew 5:11-12 (NKJV), Jesus says, "Blessed are you when they revile and persecute you, and say all kinds of evil against you *falsely* for My sake. Rejoice and be exceedingly glad, for great is your reward in heaven, for so they persecuted the prophets who were before you" (emphasis added).

There are plenty of bad things to say about me, but misogynist, bigot, homophobe, xenophobe, racist, or murderer aren't on the list. I know I'm not those things. Why should I care what they call me? I'm blessed when they say evil things against me falsely for Jesus's sake. If they're going to call you names, it's par for the course. Nobody's perfect, but the standard is still the standard. The Bible says, "Faithful are the wounds of a friend, / But the kisses of an enemy are deceitful" (Proverbs 27:6 [NKJV]).

Friends tell us the things that are hard to hear. A friend isn't going to let us continue in our sin. Not only do we need to stop apologizing for speaking the truth if we're going to overcome evil with good, we need to be confident that we know the truth.

We need to be confident.

The radical left has peddled the idea that we're full of pride and arrogance if we say we're the only ones who know the way to Heaven. Yet Jesus says, "I am the way, the truth, and the life. No one comes to the Father except through Me" (John 14:6 [NKJV]).

Do we believe that? If so, why are we ashamed of it? Paul says, "I am not ashamed of the gospel of Christ, for it is the power of God to salvation for everyone who believes" (Romans 1:16 [NKJV]).

Jesus wasn't shy in speaking the truth. The Samaritan woman says to Him, "Sir, I perceive that You are a prophet. Our fathers worshiped on this mountain, and you Jews say that in Jerusalem is the place where one ought to worship" (John 4:19 [NKJV]).

She's speaking to Jesus not as God, but as a Jewish rabbi. And Jesus responds, saying, "Woman, believe Me, the hour is coming when you will neither on this mountain, nor in Jerusalem, worship the Father. You worship what you do not know; we know what we worship, for salvation is of the Jews" (John 4:21-22 [NKJV]).

As far as she is concerned, Jesus is speaking as a Jewish man, and He is basically saying, "You have no clue what you're doing! Salvation is of the Jews. We *know* what we're talking about. We have *all* the Scriptures. We didn't do away with any of it. We didn't bring in pagan practices."

If you say something like that today, people will respond, "How arrogant of you! I can't believe you think your religion and your Jesus are the only way! You're telling me that Islam is wrong?"

You're darn right I'm telling you it's wrong.

"What about Hinduism? Buddhism? Mormonism?"

Listen, if it doesn't declare that Jesus Christ is God incarnate, that He lived a life of perfection, suffered a death on a cross, and went in the grave for three days only to resurrect Himself from the dead and send His Holy Spirit to live within anyone who would declare Him their Lord and Savior, then it's wrong! Unless they believe in that, they're going to Hell. What's wrong with us professing that? It's true. The only thing wrong with it is that our culture doesn't like it.

Jesus even goes on to say that "the hour is coming, and now is, when the true worshipers will worship the Father in spirit and truth; for the Father is seeking such to worship Him. God is Spirit, and those who worship Him must worship in spirit and truth" (John 4:23-24 [NKJV]).

Worshipping Him just in spirit isn't enough. A lot of people call themselves "spiritual beings," but they lack the understanding of what can make them spiritual. That part of a person lies dormant—spiritually dead, so to speak— waiting to be born again as the Holy Spirit indwells them.

This happens because Jesus, the Messiah, sends the truth through His Spirit to all who believe, like he does in Samaria after "The woman said to him, 'I know that Messiah is coming '(who is called Christ). 'When He comes, He will tell us all things.'"

Jesus must have smiled because He says, "I who speak to you am He'" (John 4:25-26 [NKJV]).

The fulfillment of that truth she'd been waiting for was standing right in front of her. Jesus didn't shy away from it. He wasn't embarrassed by it or ashamed of it. He simply and boldly told her what she needed to hear, and that was that.

So once we stop apologizing for speaking the truth and start finding confidence in expressing it, we need to be very aware of a basic fact when it comes to human interaction.

Not all Christians will approve of your methods.

That's a lesson I've had to learn over the course of my time in ministry, but especially as the Lord has begun the process of waking up the Church. Once Jesus had His conversation with that woman, we are told that "His disciples came, and they marveled that He talked with a woman; yet no one said, 'What do You seek? 'or, 'Why are You talking with her?'" (John 4:27 [NKJV]).

Remember the context here. A Jewish man—a rabbi, no less—with a woman. A Samaritan woman. Alone. It's scandalous! His disciples came back, they observed Jesus having that interaction with the woman, and in their minds, I'm sure they had at least initial thoughts like, "Why are you talking to her? What do you think you're doing, Jesus?" But nobody actually said that to Him. Why? Jesus had earned the respect of His disciples. Jesus had a track record of doing things that didn't make sense to them, and yet, the outcome was always good. Jesus had earned the ability to do something without them challenging Him on it.

Here's the fact. As you go out and speak truth, there are going to be other Christians who don't respect you yet. Many of them won't understand or agree with what you're doing. "Just wear the mask! Just put it on! What are you doing? Conduct your church services online, that way everybody's comfortable."

Did Jesus go around trying to please everybody? No. Quite the opposite. But He didn't seem to be concerned with that. He didn't seem to care about His own comfort level, for that matter. That's the truth. He was only concerned with accomplishing the will of the Father.

At the very beginning of this Great Awakening, some pastors publicly chastised me for remaining open. Several months later, several of those same pastors called me saying, "You know what, Pastor Tim, I'm so sorry I said those things. I want to open up my church. How did you open yours?"

In an effort to lighten the mood, I jokingly tell them, "It's easy. I go to the front door, stick my key in the lock, and turn it counterclockwise."

I had to earn their respect. Still, there are others I haven't earned respect from. Maybe I never will. That's okay. I'll just stop apologizing for speaking the truth, find confidence in expressing it, and expect that not all Christians will approve of my methods. I'll tell you what I will expect, though...

I will expect great results!

At this point in John 4:29 (NKJV), "The woman then left her waterpot, went her way into the city, and said to the men, 'Come, see a Man who told me *all things that I ever did. Could this be the Christ?* 'Then they went out of the city and came to Him" (emphasis added).

Everything she ever did. Don't miss that. This tells us there is more to the conversation than what was recorded. It went beyond the five husbands and living with a man she wasn't married to. He called her out on everything! "This man told me everything I ever did. *Everything!*"

Jesus wasn't scared of truth. He expected great results, and He got them because "Many of the Samaritans of that city believed in Him because of the word of the woman who testified, 'He told me all that I ever did. 'So when the Samaritans had come to Him, they urged Him to stay with them; and He stayed there two days. And many more believed because of His own word" (John 4:39-41 [NKJV]).

And the truth is passed on: "Then they said to the woman, 'Now we believe, not because of what you said, for we ourselves have heard Him and we know that this is indeed the Christ, the Savior of the world'" (John 4:42 [NKJV]).

One person spoke the truth to another. That person went and spoke the truth to others. Hopefully, this trend will continue.

There is an interesting scene in the eighth chapter of the book of Acts. A man named Philip "went down to the city of Samaria and preached Christ to them" (Acts 8:5 [NKJV]).

Keep in mind, this was after Jesus's death, burial, resurrection, and ascension. Acts 8:6-8 (NKJV) goes on to tell us that "the multitudes with one accord heeded the things spoken by Philip, hearing and seeing the miracles which he did. For unclean spirits, crying with a loud voice, came out of many who were possessed; and many who were paralyzed and lame were healed. And there was *great joy in that city*" (emphasis added).

My question to you is, "What city will have great joy because you determine in your heart to overcome evil with good by telling people the truth?"

8

OVERCOMING EVIL WITH GOOD BY CHALLENGING SPIRITUAL LEADERS

Spiritual leaders in America have done a very poor job engaging people with truth over the last few decades. Their desires to be liked by all and increase the size of their congregations have rendered them increasingly ineffective for the Lord, so much so that the Church was found asleep at the onset of the COVID-19 crisis. If the Church is going to move forward successfully, it must challenge its leaders to rightly divide the Word of God and boldly stand for righteousness and holiness in an environment of ever-growing darkness. The question is, "How do we challenge them in a way that honors God and honors them and the position God has placed them in?"

The first thing is, challenging them has to begin with reasonable conversations.

I'm not telling you to get in fights with pastors, yelling at them and belittling them in public. When we challenge them, we do so for their own sake and the sake of their congregations. We find a very good example of this in Acts 17:1-3 (NKJV), which says, "Now when they had passed through Amphipolis and Apollonia, they came to Thessalonica, where there was a synagogue of the Jews. Then Paul, *as his custom was*, went in to them, and for three Sabbaths *reasoned with them* from the Scriptures, explaining and demonstrating that the Christ had to suffer and rise again from the dead, and saying, 'This Jesus whom I preach to you is the Christ'" (emphasis added).

Paul traveled from place to place all over the Mediterranean region in his missionary journeys, and every time he arrived in a new city, he did the same thing. Armed with the truth of who Christ was, he went straight into the synagogues. Why? Because he always started with God's people first, primarily with the leaders of the synagogues. Paul would speak to them about their teachings and expectations. Inevitably, a good Orthodox Jew would say they'd been expecting the Messiah to come. Once he finished there, he went out into the marketplace.

The leaders in the synagogues had the writings of the prophets, and they wanted the Messiah to come and set up the kingdom. They couldn't wait for it. So Paul would open the scrolls, remind the people of the things the Messiah would achieve, and show them how Jesus did fulfill the prophesies of His birth, life, death, burial, and resurrection. He reasoned with them about the first Advent of Christ—the first coming of Christ.

As we challenge pastors today, we reason with them about the second Advent—the return of the Messiah. Many events happened some two thousand years ago that were signs of the times those Jews were living in. Those events should have made them well aware that Christ was coming the first time. In like fashion, we're living in a time where a plethora of things are happening that we've been told to look for. So when we challenge these spiritual leaders, we ask them questions like, "Didn't Peter say that scoffers would come in the last days?"

There are pastors who won't talk about the rapture of the Church, the resurrection of the dead, or the return of the Lord. They won't teach the book of Revelation at all, even though in the very beginning of Revelation 1:3 (NKJV), we're told that "*Blessed is* he who *reads* and those who *hear* the words of this prophecy, and keep those things which are written in it; for the time *is* near" (emphasis added).

They won't broach the subject. Why? Because everybody's been talking about the whole return of Christ thing, the whole rapture scenario, and the "end of the world" Armageddon stuff for years, and it just never happened. So instead of teaching people about these pressing issues, pastors brought the philosophies of the world into the pulpits of America and preached sermons like "Five ways to be the best 'you 'you can be" and other nonsense like that.

Jesus was frustrated in His first Advent. In Luke 12:54-56 (NKJV), He says to the people, "Whenever you see a cloud rising out of the west, immediately you say, 'A shower is coming'; and so it is. And when *you see* the south wind blow, you say, 'There will be hot weather'; and there is. Hypocrites! You can discern the face of the sky and of the earth, but how *is it* do not discern this time?"

Pastors need to be challenged about whether or not they can discern the times we're living in now. In listing out some of the signs for His return, Jesus tells His disciples, "For nation will rise against nation, and kingdom against kingdom" (Matthew 24:7a [NKJV]).

The word "nation" is translated from the Greek word "ethnos" in the original text, which is where we get our English word "ethnic" from. However, this is likely not the best translation, as it does not properly convey the original writer's idea. Instead, the quote should be translated to read, "For ethnicities will rise against ethnicities." We must go back to the original language to do a proper exegesis of the Scriptures. We the need to challenge pastors, asking them, "Didn't Jesus say that there would come a point in time when ethnic groups were going to fight with ethnic groups?" At a time when critical race theory is being introduced at the kindergarten level in most public schools across our nation, shouldn't we know this is a sign? The Black Lives Matter movement is infiltrating practically every bank and major corporation. They've even infiltrated churches with their radical critical race theory. As a result, many people, whether knowingly or unknowingly, are misled into believing that supporting Black Lives Matter is a virtuous thing to do. But it pits people against one another based on race, and by partaking in it, people are advancing the cause of the spirit of antichrist and pushing us closer to the second Advent of Christ.

Some churches are even demanding that others follow their example of writing out statements against racism. I know this because I've received their demands over email. My mom always told me that actions speak louder than words. Here's a novel idea: just don't be racist! Why do I need to tell people I'm not? How is it that these spiritual leaders are demanding we make these types of Marxist statements, and no one is challenging them on it? Someone needs to say to them, "Wait a minute. Don't you see this is prophetic? How could you partake in that?"

In Matthew 24:7b (NKJV), didn't Jesus also say that "there will be famines, pestilences, and earthquakes in various places?"

Why aren't spiritual leaders telling people this is an absolute, unequivocal sign that we're near the return of Christ? The truth is, if a pastor does speak up and address the COVID-19 crisis for what it is (a clear sign), that pastor is shamed by other undiscerning pastors. They say things like, "Oh, those pastors who are opening their churches are a danger to society. Those pastors think it's an attack on the

Church. It's not an attack. It's just a virus, and we're going to have to get through this."

Well, is it a virus that's deadly? Yes. People *can* die from it. People *have* died from it. Is it a virus that's affecting the whole world? Yes. So does that mean it's a pestilence, a pandemic? Yes. Didn't Jesus tell us to look for this? Yes.

"Then pastor, why aren't you telling your congregation that?"

Didn't Jesus also say that before He came back, we'd be living in times when mass deception would take place? In fact, He warned us to "Take heed that no one deceives you" (Matthew 24:4 [NKJV]).

Aren't we living in a time when deception is commonplace? Terms like "fake news" and "fact check" have become so prevalent they have lost their effectiveness. Many people will believe just about anything you place in front of them on social media, true or untrue. Pastors need to be asked, "Why aren't you talking about these things? Why aren't you equipping your congregation with methods for dealing with and responding to this? Why aren't you showing them this is one of the signs of the imminent return of Christ?"

They need to be challenged on these things because they're not doing their congregation any good. They're misleading massive amounts of people. God didn't wake us up to allow that to continue. These weak, undiscerning spiritual leaders have gone unchecked for too long. We must challenge them with reasonable conversations.

These challenges will bear fruit. I am proof.

Notice that as Paul reasons with the spiritual leaders in the synagogues in Acts 17:4 (NKJV), "some of them were persuaded; and a great multitude of the devout Greeks, and not a few of the leading women, joined Paul and Silas."

Some are going to believe it, and the act of challenging will change their lives. It changed mine. As I mentioned in the introduction to this book, God had to wake me up, and He used a few key circumstances in my life to challenge me and open my eyes to what was happening to the Church. This challenge radically changed my ministry. My goals and expectations changed. Even my preaching changed. The challenge was good for me, and it is good for other pastors as well. The more you do it, the more fruit you will see. There's another thing you need to be aware of, however.

Challenging spiritual leaders will earn you some adversaries.

I guarantee some people are going to oppose you. They opposed Paul. Some were persuaded.

But the Jews who were not persuaded, *becoming envious,* took some of the evil men from the marketplace, and gathering a mob, set all the city in an uproar and attacked the house of Jason, and sought to bring them out to the people. But when they did not find them, they dragged Jason and some brethren to the rulers of the city, crying out, "These who have turned the world upside down have come here too. Jason has harbored them, and these are all acting contrary to the decrees of Caesar, saying there is another king—Jesus." And they troubled the crowd and the rulers of the city when they heard these things. So when they had taken security from Jason and the rest, they let them go. (Acts 17:5-9 [NKJV])

There are three very important things we need to recognize in these verses. First, the ones who were not persuaded became envious. For the people who received the truth, their lives were changed, and they went with Paul. The spiritual leaders who were left behind became envious of Paul. Why? Because Paul had the truth, which is very attractive, and those who were persuaded by it weren't going to stay with those who weren't.

Second, truth exposes false teachings and teachers. When you shed its light on false doctrines or their propagators, they're exposed for who and what they are.

And what do envious spiritual leaders do? Today, they're resorting to the same tactics of those envious leaders of Paul's day. They get evil men from the marketplace. In other words, they go out into the world and join forces with evil people. They form a mob, which is why you have pastors taking a knee at Black Lives Matter protests; they have a mob mentality just like the men in the time of Paul.

Once the truth is out, and the wicked leaders are exposed, they attack the people who are bringing the truth as if they're the ones doing something wrong. And notice that they brought an accusation against the bearers of truth that they were "acting contrary to the decrees of Caesar." They joined together with a mob, and they sided with the government of man instead of the government of God. The finger of accusation goes to the person who's bringing truth. I've heard it. I've had the envious leaders tell me, "I can't believe you opened up your church. You're going against the rules Gavin Newsom gave us!"

My answer to that claim is, "I don't care!"

Those of us who have the Holy Spirit in us are dual citizens. In Philippians 3:20-21 (NKJV), Paul says, "*our citizenship is in heaven,* from which we also eagerly wait for the Savior, the Lord Jesus Christ, who will transform our lowly body that it may be conformed to His glorious body, according to the working by which He is able even to subdue all things to Himself" (emphasis added).

It's not on earth. If you have been born again of the Holy Spirit, you have entered into the kingdom of Heaven. You've entered into eternity. You're now a citizen of Heaven, and as such, you have a dual citizenship. There's the government of Heaven and the government of whatever country you hail from. The form of government in America is a republic. The government in Heaven is a monarchy where God is king. Both of these governments currently exist simultaneously, but one of them has a higher power. But the spiritual leaders who grow envious and reject the truth end up siding with the lower one.

Many of you may have already experienced this is some form or another. I've had many people approach me telling me their own family members have sided with the governments of man instead of God, saying, "If you're going to go to church, you're not welcome over at our house." It's a sad thing.

Remember, Paul went straight to the synagogue to get started with God's people first. While Jason was dealing with the envious Jews, "the brethren immediately sent Paul and Silas away by night to Berea. When they arrived, they went into the synagogue of the Jews" (Acts 17:10 [NKJV]).

The town he was in—Berea—was an interesting place with unique people who brought out something very special about challenging spiritual leaders. While it's for their own good and the good of their congregation, there's another aspect of it we don't want to miss.

Challenging spiritual leaders has more to do with you than it does with them.

We challenge them because we love them. We want them to be aware of what's going on, teach what's right, and lead their congregations in strength. If they respond well to the challenge, it means they're healthy pastors, which in turn creates a healthy congregation, community, state, and country. But in actuality, challenging them doesn't really have to do with them. It's more about you.

In Acts 17:11 (NKJV), as Paul reasons with the Bereans in their synagogue, he notes that they "were more *fair-minded* than those in Thessalonica, in that they received the word with all readiness, and searched the Scriptures daily *to find out* whether these things were so" (emphasis added).

According to Paul, the Bereans are "fair-minded." This translation comes from the Greek word "eugenes" in the original text, which conveys the idea of having a noble mind. The word "noble" means having a fine or excellent personal quality. How did they achieve that type of standing in Paul's mind? They "received the Word with all readiness." When we receive the Word of God, it works effectively in us as we believe. It literally does something in us when we take it in through our eyes or ears.

Not only did they receive the Word with readiness, but Paul also records that they "searched the Scriptures daily to find out whether these things were so." The tables had turned. The Bereans were challenging Paul. They weren't going to take Paul's word for it. They were going to consult the Word of God and make sure that what Paul was telling them lined up with what God had already said in His Word.

I want to encourage you to do the same thing. Be a Berean. Don't just take my word for it. Don't just take your pastor's word for it. Search the Scriptures every single day. I frequently tell my congregation when they go home on a Sunday to make sure I taught them right. And if they find I didn't, I tell them to run, and run fast! (But to at least challenge me first). I tell them that they owe it to themselves, they owe it to their family, and they owe it to their community to make sure they're being taught right.

Challenging spiritual leaders begs the question, "What type of person do you want to be?" Are you going to be that type of person that's tossed around by every wind of doctrine? There are enough people like that already. Are you going to be that type of person? Or are you going to be the type of person who has a mind of your own and utilizes your critical thinking skills?

9

OVERCOMING EVIL WITH GOOD BY HOLDING GOVERNMENT OFFICIALS ACCOUNTABLE

You may remember in June 2020, St. John's Episcopal Church, which is just across the street from the White House, was set on fire. That church, established in 1816, is known as the "church of presidents." It was set ablaze during violent riots that ensued in response to the killing of George Floyd by a member of the Minneapolis Police Department.

Beautiful history was set on fire as a form of retaliation for the horrific thing that took place in Minneapolis. The Secret Service had to rush President Trump to a bunker under the White House because of the violence until the riots subsided. Afterward, he walked across the street with Bible in hand for a photo op. In the picture, he's holding up the Bible; it went viral. In response, House Speaker Nancy Pelosi created her own photo op in which she quoted a very small section from chapter three of the book of Ecclesiastes.

Nancy Pelosi, the current Speaker of the House, is a woman who frequently makes mention of her Catholic faith. As Fr. Mark Hodges explains in his article for LifeSiteNews written on June 2, 2015, "Pelosi, who described herself as a faithful Christian and 'mainstream Catholic, 'said her pre-adolescent grandchildren needed to see and be present at a gay and lesbian celebration in order 'to give them the image that we have for all people.'"[24]

---

24. Mark Hodges, "Nancy Pelosi: Gay 'marriage' is 'consistent' with Catholic teaching," LifeSiteNews, accessed June 2, 2015, https://www.lifesitenews.com/news/nancy-pelosi-gay-marriage-is-consistent-with-catholic-teaching.

She goes on to explain that same-sex marriage "is important," and that her grandchildren "have been hearing this [message supporting gay marriage] their whole life" because "they go to Catholic school."[25]

The Catholic doctrine makes it clear that marriage is between one man and one woman. Additionally, according to the Catholic faith, abortion is an egregious sin. Apparently, she was absent the day they taught that in her Catechism class as a child because she has been a champion for abortion rights her entire political career.

To be blunt, Nancy Pelosi should not call herself a Catholic. She should refrain from using the Word of God in her political office as a means of attacking her opponent. She isn't alone either. There are countless politicians whose feet need to be held to the fire.

Not only should many politicians be kicked out of the Church, but the government should have no part or say in what the Church does at all due to the separation of Church

---

25. Hodges, "Gay marriage is consistent."

and State. Contrary to popular belief, America didn't come up with the idea.

It is by His design that the separation would exist. America was founded on principles from the Word of God, and this is one of those principles God expects humanity to follow. If the Church is going to overcome the evil in our culture, it must challenge government officials, especially ones who fly the banner of Christianity. And there is one thing true about doing that.

Holding government officials accountable is easy—now.

It really is easy right now, but in the future, it might not be. Jesus tells us in Luke 21:12-13 (NKJV) about a time in the future that the government "will lay their hands on you and persecute you, delivering you up to the synagogues and prisons. You will be brought before kings and rulers for My name's sake."

No matter the form of persecution, the end goal is to get the Christians to shut up. The misuse of the legal system and the power of social media platforms are being used to silence the voice of Christians and conservatives in America; however, we're not yet at the point when we'll be "brought before kings and rulers." But that time is approaching fast.

What's taking place on a nation-wide scale right now is the implementation of laws that will enable the government to exercise that type of control over a person's life. Case in point is Assembly Bill A416 from the State of New York, which "Relates to the removal of cases, contacts and carriers of communicable diseases who are potentially dangerous to the public health."[26]

As you read the language in this Bill, and you see what the desired additions to the public health law are, you'll find that it sounds like a lost chapter from *The Hunger Games.*

Section 1 of the Bill states, "The public health law is amended by adding a new section 2120-a to read as follows: Upon determining by clear and convincing evidence that the health of others is or may be endangered by a case, contact

---

26. Assembly Bill A416, New York S., (2021), Section 2, https://www.nysenate.gov/legislation/bills/2021/a416.

or carrier, or suspected case, contact or carrier of a contagious disease, the governor or his or her delegee, including, but not limited to the commissioner or the heads of local health departments, may order the removal and/or detention of such a person or of a group of such persons by issuing a single order."[27]

"*May* be endangered" is pretty ambiguous. What about "suspected" cases? That word takes away liability from the one making the determination. And who gets to determine?

So let's just play a game of hypotheticals for a moment. A group of churchgoers attends church on a Sunday morning. The governor, who may not be agreeable to churches holding services, says the church members "may" be a threat because he "suspects" that one of them "may" have come in contact with a disease. According to New York Assembly Bill A416, that group of Christians can be removed and detained "in a medical facility or other

---

27. Assembly Bill A416

appropriate facility or premises designated by the governor or his or her delegee."[28]

Well, what's "appropriate?" Is jail appropriate? At the onset of the COVID-19 crisis, members of the radical left deemed it inappropriate to keep prisoners locked up and demanded that rapists, child molesters, and the like be let out of the jails and back out on the streets. Their reasoning? Keeping them incarcerated was placing them at risk of harm from the virus.[29] Watch how fast those tables turn if it's determined that Christians "may" have come in contact with someone who "may" have had a contagious disease.

Another passage in this Bill that reeks of communism states, "In no event shall any person be detained for more than sixty days without a court order authorizing such

---

28. Assembly Bill A416

29. Josh Campbell, "These 'high risk' California sex offenders were released early. A prosecutor warns they're still a threat," CNN Wire Service, (May 8, 2020), https://www.mercurynews.com/2020/05/08/these-high-risk-california-sex-offenders-were-released-early-a-prosecutor-warns-theyre-still-a-threat/.

detention."[30] This was unfathomable in the early 2000s. Now, it's a clear and present danger.

Additionally, according to this Bill, if there are treatments you don't want to expose your body to, such as vaccinations, they can "require an individual who has been exposed to or infected by a contagious disease to complete an appropriate, prescribed course of treatment, preventive medication or vaccination, including directly observed therapy to treat the disease."[31]

"Directly observed?" Talk about creepy! They want to watch! Satan's fingerprint is all over this Bill. He would love nothing more than to watch as your human rights are being violated. And don't even think about causing a ruckus or trying to escape! They have declared that "a person who is detained in a medical facility, or other appropriate facility or premises, shall not conduct himself or herself in a disorderly manner, and shall not leave or attempt to leave such facility

---

30. Assembly Bill A416
31. Assembly Bill A416

or premises until he or she is discharged pursuant to this section."

Bills like this will pass and be placed into law all around the nation. Do you know how I know that? Because Satan has done a really good job of instilling fear in everyone. And when people are afraid, you can control them.

A person who has a relationship with Jesus need not fear. Actually, when it does come to the point that Christians are brought before the leaders of government "it will turn out for you as an occasion for testimony. Therefore settle it in your hearts not to meditate beforehand on what you will answer; for I will give you a mouth and wisdom which all your adversaries will not be able to contradict or resist" (Luke 21:13-15 [NKJV]).

In other words, God is going to speak right through you. You don't have to predetermine what you're going to say. This type of environment can turn people against each other. Sometimes, the betrayal comes from those who are considered the least likely to turn their backs on a loved one.

Jesus says, "You will be betrayed even by parents and brothers, relatives and friends; and they will put some of you to death" (Luke 21:13-16 [NKJV]).

Again, we're pushing ourselves toward that. On April 10, 2020, the city of Riverside, California, published a statement on their website titled "Riverside County launches mobile app to report nonessential businesses." In that statement, Fourth District Supervisor Chair V. Manuel Perez justified the implementation of the app by saying, "We must mitigate and suppress the spread of the coronavirus. This app will help identify hotspots that will lead to efficiently responding to businesses that are risking the health of the community." Additionally,

> RivCoMobile—which also provides services and information to residents—has a "Coronavirus" feature on the landing page. This will be used to make anonymous reports about possible violations of orders issued by the State of California or the County of Riverside public health officer. These violations

may include the operation of nonessential businesses, unauthorized gatherings and failure by essential businesses to comply with health orders such as facial coverings and social distancing for staff or patrons. The new feature will provide critical data to Riverside University Health System health officials, who track and address the spread of COVID-19 in Riverside County.[32]

"Unauthorized gatherings." At the time, that included upcoming Easter celebrations, weddings, funerals, or even a neighborhood block party. They implemented a way to anonymously turn in friends, family, neighbors, and coworkers. People who died alone were buried alone. Funerals were cancelled, either for fear of contracting the COVID-19 virus or being anonymously reported to the government.

---

32. News Staff. "Riverside county launches mobile app to report nonessential businesses," NBC Palm Springs, (April 10, 2020), https://nbcpalmsprings.com/2020/04/10/riverside-county-launches-mobile-app-to-report-nonessential-businesses/.

Riverside, California was not the exception. Tattletale apps like theirs quickly became commonplace. America entered a new era of self-policing that eerily resembles the tactics of the Nazis in 1933. According to *Holocaust and Human Behavior*, a Facing History and Ourselves Publication, "As the Nazis worked to consolidate their power and build a cohesive 'national community,' suppression of dissent played a key role. In 1933, the Nazis issued a decree that required Germans to turn in anyone who spoke against the party, its leaders, or the government."[33] Of course, the use of apps like that of Riverside County are optional; however, people are being conditioned to accept this as a normal part of our culture. Remember the law of incrementalism we discussed in chapter seven? It's happening right before our eyes.

As a child, I wondered how the world could ever get that bad. Now I see how it can. This is why if we're going to move forward and overcome the evil in this world with

---

33. "Spying on Family and Friends," *Holocaust and Human Behavior*, (Facing History and Ourselves, accessed February 12, 2021), https://www.facinghistory.org/holocaust-and-human-behavior/chapter-6/spying-family-and-friends.

good, we're going to have to get involved and hold these government officials accountable. They probably won't like it. In fact, they may even hate us. In Luke 21:17-18 (NKJV), Jesus says, "*you will be hated* by all for My name's sake. But not a hair of your head shall be lost" (emphasis added).

Remember, this is a time in the future, but that future is fast approaching! Christians will be hated. Jesus warned it would happen. We need to understand this, accept it, and embrace it. If you live life the way a Christian is supposed to, the world is going to hate you.

Our eyes are now open to this. The government wants us to be dependent on and beholden to it. It hates Jesus, and because we have the Holy Spirit of Jesus in us, it hates us, too. We need to stand strong against this by holding government officials accountable, and it's easy—now. But we also need to understand something else.

Holding government officials accountable is part of God's designed order.

2 Chronicles gives us an account of a king named Uzziah. He was made king when he was just sixteen years old, and his reign lasted for fifty-two years. As a teenager, though, he lacked experience and wisdom, so God was with him and strengthened him. With God's help, King Uzziah became successful and famous in the land. But sometimes fame goes to one's head, and they can develop an attitude that says, "I don't need God anymore. I've got this." That's exactly what happened with young King Uzziah. We're told, "when he was strong his heart was lifted up, to his destruction, for he transgressed against the LORD his God by entering the temple of the LORD to burn incense on the altar of incense" (2 Chronicles 26:16 [NKJV]). Similarly, there are a lot of people who start out well in government. They get elected to office with great intentions to help the people they're supposed to serve. With that office, however, comes power and authority—two things that, if utilized improperly, can ruin a person and make them think they don't need God.

At first glance it doesn't seem like Uzziah did anything wrong. After all, he was burning incense on the altar of incense. Isn't that a good thing? Absolutely. But that's not the question to ask. The correct question is, "Was it his job?" The answer? No. He was the king, not the priest.

In ancient Israel, there were three offices ordained by God. Prophets, priests, and kings. Three uniquely different and separate roles. The role of a king was to run the government affairs and oversee the army. Priests were men of the lineage of Aaron and handled the affairs of the temple. They represented the people to God, making atonement for the sins of the people through prescribed sacrifices. Prophets were the ones who represented God to the people. If God had something to say, He would speak it to the prophets, and the prophets would convey it.

These three separate offices weren't to be intermingled. One person could not hold all three jobs. That didn't take place until much later when Christ was the prophet of all prophets, the priest of all priests, and the king of all kings. What happened in the life of Uzziah, and it happens all too often with government officials today, is that his pride was lifted up to the point where he wanted total power and control. He didn't want to be limited to overseeing the affairs of the government; he wanted control over what took place at the temple. Does that sound familiar at all? Government officials in America don't just want to have power and authority in the government, they want power and authority over the Church as well. That's not a part of God's design. Uzziah, like many in American politics today, was seeking an office that wasn't his to seek. He'd already been given a role by God and should have stuck with it. According to 2 Chronicles 26:17 (NKJV), in response to Uzziah's actions, "Azariah the priest went in after him, and with him were eighty priests of the LORD—*valiant men*" (emphasis added).

Keep in mind, a king can have somebody executed, so that was risky for Azariah and his valiant men. I'm sure they were a bit apprehensive about it, but they did it nonetheless. They went in after the king because the king was doing something wrong.

How many spiritual leaders today can be described as valiant men? Sadly, not many. We need manly pastors likened to the Black Robe Regiment during the American Revolutionary War who promoted American independence—brave men who will do exactly what Azariah and those eighty other priests did. We are told that "they withstood King Uzziah, and said to him, 'It is not for you, Uzziah, to burn incense to the LORD, but for the priests, the sons of Aaron, who are consecrated to burn incense. Get out of the sanctuary, for you have trespassed! You shall have no honor from the LORD God" (2 Chronicles 26:17-18 [NKJV]).

Pastors filled with the Holy Spirit and backed by their congregations need to boldly tell the government to get out of the affairs of the Church. They need to be told that they have no role in what happens there. They need to be told, and we need to be prepared that they will not like it. As Azariah was taking his bold stance against the king, "Uzziah became furious; and he had a censer in his hand to burn incense. And while he was angry with the priests, leprosy broke out on his forehead, before the priests in the house of the LORD, beside the incense altar" (2 Chronicles 26:19 [NKJV]).

Of course he became furious. Those in positions of authority never like being challenged. Because of the power they wield, most people are reluctant to do so anyway. That is certainly the case in American politics.

Several years ago, I founded Our Watch with Tim Thompson, a non-profit organization that's purpose is to help shed some light on the wickedness around us. One of the first things that ministry did was call local school districts to find out what was being taught regarding sex education. One district in California told us they were about to release the new curriculum, and they were having an informational meeting to show parents what would be taught. When asked how many parents typically attend those types of meetings, their response was very alarming. They said they usually have about twenty-five parents in attendance. Keep in mind, this is a California public school with thousands of students, but only about twenty-five parents cared enough to show up. So I called every single pastor in that city and invited them all to attend and encourage the members of their congregations to attend as well. How many of those pastors do you think showed up? One. We did have about one hundred and sixty people show up, though. That's a whole lot better than twenty-five.

The entire city should have been in an uproar because the government was influencing the position of the Church. The Church equips the parents, who in turn teach the children. The government has no business teaching our children about sexuality. Let me be clear, I'm not talking about the "birds and the bees" kind of stuff you may have been introduced to when you were a kid. That's biology. The school can teach biology all day long as far as I care. If they want to teach that the sperm meets the egg, cells divide and attach to the uterus, a baby develops, etc., that's fine. But that's not what they're teaching in American public schools.

For the sake of keeping this book PG-13, I will spare you the disgusting details. Just know that what they are teaching is not sex education—it's "sexuality training." They're teaching children how to give and receive consent for sexual experiences—how to experiment with various types of sexual acts that cross the entire LGBTQ+ spectrum. They offer various resources to the teenagers who seek to undermine the authority of their parents, the Church, and the Word of God. One of those resources is teensource.org. Children sign up for texts, and it sends them weekly messages. For example, in a text message they sent out in January 2021, the teens are told that "The CDC (Centers for Disease Control and Prevention) recently estimated that 1 in 5 people has an STD, that is to say, they are very common!"

When you listen to their language, it becomes very clear that they are trying to normalize sexual activity among our youth. Another thing that is clear, especially for a person who has trained their ear to discern when someone is trying to lead people astray, is that their message literally tells the child the opposite of God's Word. For example, that same message goes on to say, "STDs are *not something to feel ashamed of*, but if left untreated, some of them can cause things like pelvic pain or infertility (the inability to have a baby in the future), so it is important to learn how to prevent, get tested for, and treat STDs. Even though we are practicing social distancing due to COVID-19, our tips for protecting yourself from STDs are important whenever you have sex, now or in the future."[34]

Not something to be ashamed of? In speaking of His people during a time of rebellion in Jeremiah 6:15 (NKJV), God says, "*Were they ashamed* when they had committed abomination? / No! They were not at all ashamed; / *Nor did they know how to blush.* / Therefore they shall fall among those who fall; / At the time I punish them, / They shall be cast down'" (emphasis added).

The sexualization of our children is creating an environment where anything goes. A culture that doesn't know how to blush. Modesty is thrown out the window, and lascivious behavior is celebrated. This is what happens when the government takes the place of the Church, and it needs to be challenged. However, we don't have eighty valiant spiritual leaders like Azariah had. Reading the account of Uzziah's sin makes me wonder how long it would have gone

---

34. "Teen Health Resources & Information," TeenSource, (accessed February 12, 2021), https://www.teensource.org/.

on if Azariah and those eighty priests didn't go in and put a stop to it. How long would Uzziah have been able to take the place of the priests? Would it have ever stopped? When you think about it, if those priests never did what they did, the story of Israel would be drastically different today. So, what about the story of America?

Remember, holding government officials accountable is easy—now. And it's part of God's designed order. We need godly, valiant pastors to lead in this. But there is something else to keep in mind.

It's not just the role of the pastors; it's the role of all believers.

In fact, God has made you a king and a priest. In the first chapter of the book of Revelation we are told that "from Jesus Christ, the faithful witness, the firstborn from the dead, and the ruler over the kings of the earth" (Revelation 1:5 [NKJV]).

Revelation 1: 5-6 (NKJV) also tells us, "To Him who loved us and washed us from our sins in His own blood, and *has made us kings and priests* to His God and Father, to Him be glory and dominion forever and ever. Amen" (emphasis added).

Who is "us?" The Church. God has called upon the Church to act as kings in the sense that we govern our own spirits and judge the earth. Christ is coming back, and when He does, He's bringing us with Him. He's going to rule from Jerusalem, and we get to help. God has also called upon the Church to act as priests. We represent the people to God. We offer sacrifice. Because of this call on our lives, we are well-qualified to hold government officials accountable.

The social conditioning that is taking place is instilling in people a warped understanding of the government's role in their lives. People are willfully giving up their rights one by one and being moved closer to fascism every day. Our children and grandchildren depend upon us taking action now. If there is to be an America for them to grow up in and have opportunities to flourish as we had, the battles need to be fought, and they will not be fought from the couch.

10

DEVELOPING A NEW APPROACH

It has been the intent of this book to address the Church's sleepiness, its response to what happened to it, and to offer suggestions for how it can take a very active role in overcoming evil with good by utilizing a threefold strategy:

1. Speak truth into the lives of others

2. Challenge "spiritual leaders"

3. Hold government officials accountable, especially the ones who fly the banner of Christianity

In various ways, the Church may have been engaging in those three activities on some level or another. If I'm right, and we're in the midst of America's Final Great Awakening, the Church is going to have to develop a new approach to implementing that strategy and addressing the cultural issues of our day. If we're honest with ourselves, what we have been doing isn't working. It's time for a change.

In the 2016 presidential election, I voted for Donald Trump. My decision to vote for him rested solidly on three of his campaign promises. First, he said he would move the U.S. Embassy from Tel Aviv to Jerusalem, the eternal capital of the Jewish people. In 1995, the U.S. Congress passed the Jerusalem Embassy Act, which stated that the United States Embassy in Israel should be established in Jerusalem no later than May 31, 1999. Every six months during the presidencies of Bill Clinton, George W. Bush, and Barack Obama, a waiver was signed to keep the U.S. Embassy in Tel Aviv, citing national security reasons. The second campaign promise made by Donald Trump that secured my vote for him was that he would place conservative justices on the Supreme Court of the United States. The third was his commitment to life, claiming he would prohibit the use of taxpayer dollars to fund abortion.

His opponent, Hillary Clinton, didn't run on those kinds of promises. I voted for him, and thankfully, he won. I say thankfully, because he made good on those promises. On December 6, 2017, he announced the United States ' recognition of Jerusalem as the capital of Israel, and he ordered the planning of the relocation of the U.S. Embassy in Israel from Tel Aviv to Jerusalem. He made three appointments to the Supreme Court: Neil Gorsuch in April 2017, Brett Kavanaugh in October 2018, and Amy Coney Barrett in October 2020. Also, he emerged to be, in my humble opinion, the most pro-life president America has ever known.

The second time around, in the 2020 presidential elections, for the reasons previously mentioned, I voted for Donald Trump again. Sadly, in an environment plagued with allegations of fraud, he did not come out victorious. Four years of winning seemed to end abruptly, and the proverbial wind in the sails of Bible-believing, freedom-loving Americans were silenced. Millions of voters cast their ballots to see what was dubbed as the MAGA (Make America Great Again) movement continue on in victory, but on January 20, 2021, they sat in the stillness of apparent defeat as they watched Joe Biden be sworn in as the forty-sixth president of the United States.

Developing a new strategy to be effective for God's plan often becomes necessary after a time of great defeat.

In Luke 16:1-2 (NKJV), Jesus uses a parable to teach His disciples. He says, "There was a certain rich man who had a steward, and an accusation was brought to him that this man was wasting his goods. So he called him and said to him, 'What is this I hear about you? Give an account of your stewardship, for *you can no longer be steward*'" (emphasis added).

In the infamous words of the forty-fifth president of the United States, "You're fired!" If you've ever been fired, you know how that man would have felt. Losing a job is embarrassing. It's a feeling of defeat that only those who have experienced it can know.

Remember, this is a parable. An earthly story with a Heavenly meaning. So in this earthly story, the master is God, and the steward is us. We're all stewards. Why? Because the Holy Spirit and the Gospel of Jesus have been placed into us. God has entrusted us to use them wisely here on earth. The steward in this story didn't use the master's property wisely. He was wasting the resources that his master had given him, and the master called him into account.

Following the 2020 elections, I had to remind my fellow Christians we may have lost that battle, but we aren't fighting to win the war. The war has already been fought. It's done. It was over roughly two thousand years ago when Jesus Christ was resurrected from the dead. I had to encourage people not to let the feeling of defeat get them down. They needed to know that the fact is, when we lose a battle, it's time for us to revise our strategy.

A new strategy will be much more effective and likely to succeed if we accept our weaknesses.

According to Luke 16:3-4 (NKJV), in response to being fired, "the steward said within himself, 'What shall I do? For my master is taking the stewardship away from me. *I cannot dig*; I am ashamed to beg. I have resolved what to do, that when I am put out of the stewardship, they may receive me into their houses'" (emphasis added).

That steward knew his weaknesses couldn't be part of his plan to move forward. As the Church strategizes our future approach to ministry, we have to recognize and accept our areas of weakness. God has given each and every one of us some sort of spiritual gift. We need to know what that is, then do it. We need to stay away from the areas we're *not* gifted in. Trying to be strong in our areas of weakness causes us to end up spinning our wheels and getting us nowhere.

Our new approach should utilize the resources that are at our disposal.

Notice that the steward "called every one of his master's debtors to *him*, and said to the first, 'How much do you owe my master? 'And he said, 'A hundred measures of oil'" (Luke 16:5-6 [NKJV]).

The steward shows great mercy and tells the debtor, "'Take your bill, and sit down quickly and write fifty.'" His generosity doesn't end there; he continues to reduce their debts: "Then he said to another, 'And how much do you owe? 'So he said, 'A hundred measures of wheat'" (Luke 16:7 [NKJV]).

The kindly steward replies, "'Take your bill, and write eighty'" (Luke 16:7 [NKJV]).

At first glance, these verses appear to suggest that this steward just ripped off his master. Understand that there are three main ways people explain this. The first, and I think the most *unlikely* one, is that the steward was in fact stealing from the master. I say unlikely because in the next verse, the master commends him for his shrewdness. Remember, the master is God, the steward is us. Do you think for a second that if we go out and cheat God out of what is His, He's going to respond with a commendation? Probably not.

The second explanation is the steward could have been removing the accrued interest from the bill.

Deuteronomy 23:20 (NKJV) tells us the law mandated that "To a foreigner you may charge interest, but to your brother you shall *not charge interest*, that the LORD your God may bless you in all to which you set your hand in the land which you are entering to possess" (emphasis added).

The Bible doesn't tell us what authority he used. It just says he used it, and the master commended him for it.

The third explanation most commonly provided is the steward simply removed his own commission. As a steward, he was allowed to make investments on the master's behalf, and in turn, make a living from it. So maybe he cut his commission off.

I believe he either removed his commission or the interest. Either he was using the law to his advantage, or he was willing to exercise personal sacrifice. Both of those would have been resources at his disposal, and each would gain a commendation from the master.

The Church's new approach needs to utilize the resources it has. Following the 2020 election, a multitude of lawsuits were filed against the various registrars of voters across America. Those lawsuits and future suits of that nature are vital to the success of the Church moving forward. Why? Because every two years, there's an election in America. The Church needs to be very strategic in how it approaches these elections.

Our strategy has to involve personal sacrifice. That may mean some of you reading this will have to run for public office. Every two years, there are seats on the city council and school board that are up for grabs. That means in a four-year period, every seat will have gone through a change, or it will have stayed exactly how it was. The Church needs to look at every single seat of every elected position in its city, and it needs to ensure that a strong, conservative Christian is elected to these seats. Running for office as a true believer is a great personal sacrifice. You'll find yourself in the lion's den. People will say all sorts of wicked things about you that aren't true.

For some of you, it means you're going to have to homeschool your kids. Until we get solid believers on our school boards, the public school system is going to remain the indoctrination factory of the radical left.

Our new approach will need to put the *"whatever it takes"* mindset on steroids.

Notice that in Luke 16:8 (NKJV), "the master commended the unjust steward because he had dealt shrewdly. For the sons of this world are more shrewd in their generation than the sons of light."

To be shrewd means you find a way to make it happen. Remember that a lot of people who have read this parable think this steward ripped off his master, but that's only how it appears. Know this: as you are shrewd, others are going to see your actions and immediately think the worst of you just as with the steward. I have personally experienced this.

Years ago, Our Watch with Tim Thompson created a documentary that exposed how the ACLU and a company called Cardea Services was instructing California school district employees how to ensure our daughters can get an abortion without us knowing and how to teach our children sexually perverse curriculums by doing all they can to ensure parents have no way to opt their children out.[35]

We accomplished this by going undercover to one of the instructional meetings. Do you know how we got into the meeting? We lied. We outright lied. We sent two people in with covert cameras, each with made up stories about who they were and why they were there. When the documentary came out, some Christians came to me and asked how we got into the meetings to capture the footage. When I told them we lied, I had several people say things like, "You lied? Pastor Tim, you shouldn't have done that. Two wrongs don't make a right. You've totally discredited

35. "NO OPT-OUT ALLOWED: The California Sex Ed Indoctrination." (June 26, 2019, Uploaded by Jeremiah Films, Vimeo, 31:32), https://vimeo.com/344632997.

yourself and the documentary because you're a part of a lie now."

Think about it for a moment. We got in. We exposed what they were doing. People are now better informed so they can make good decisions for their families. I'd lie ten times more if I had to in order to make sure wicked people can't treat our kids this way! I couldn't believe my ears. I was like, "Would you just read the Bible?"

As you read the lineage of Jesus in chapter one of Matthew's Gospel, you'll learn about Rahab. She was a prostitute who *lied* to save some of God's people, and God blessed her with the eternal privilege of being in His Word as somebody who was in the line of Jesus Christ. She lied, and God blessed her for it. Why? Because it advanced the cause of the Kingdom of God. Now don't get me wrong, I'm not saying we should be liars. As Christians, we need to be people of truth, but we also need to be shrewd. We need to know what must be done and find a way to make it happen.

This may mean we'll have to do things that we normally wouldn't do. It's a rare thing that I would ever call somebody a racist. The radical left throws that word around like a beach ball at a concert. They've owned the definition of what a racist is, and now they call people a racist for things that aren't racist. Guess what? It works. We need to start calling them racists. Think about the concept of school choice. To most Bible-believing Christians, school choice makes a lot of sense. The concept is simple. Say, for instance, that a public school is given thirteen thousand dollars per student, per calendar year, to be at their school. If school choice were a reality, that thirteen thousand dollars would be given to the parent to use at a school of their choice.

Truth be told, public schools are horrible, but in predominantly black communities, they're even worse. We need push for school choice. When the radical left pushes back, we call them racists. We need to take out political ads exposing their disdain for the black community. Why wouldn't they want them to have the option of sending their child down the street to a better school? They don't have people calling *them* racist, do they? They're the ones playing that card. And guess what? They're winning. They're winning because we're just doing the same thing over and over again, and we never change it up.

The parable Jesus used has to do with how you and I are going to be received into the Kingdom. Jesus says:

make friends for yourselves by unrighteous mammon, that when you fail, they may receive you into an everlasting home. He who is faithful in what is least is faithful also in much; and he who is unjust in what is least is unjust also in much. Therefore if you have not been faithful in the unrighteous mammon, who will commit to your trust the true riches? And if you have not been faithful in what is another man's, who will give you what is your own?

No servant can serve two masters; for either he will hate the one and love the other, or else he will be loyal to the one and despise the other. You cannot serve God and mammon. (Luke 16:9-13 [NKJV])

God has placed within us the Gospel of Jesus Christ and His Holy Spirit. He's entrusted us with earthly riches and opportunities and wants us to faithfully use them to advance the cause of the kingdom of God here on earth because what we have after this is so much greater. So while there's still breath in us, let's be wise, let's be shrewd, and let's accomplish much for Jesus. The rapture of the Church could happen at any moment. If it does, praise God! If it doesn't, we've got work to do. God didn't wake us up to go right back to sleep. He woke us up for a purpose. We can no longer ride the fence of indecisiveness. We can no longer lounge on the couch of procrastination.

Moses asks God, "Indeed, when I come to the children of Israel and say to them, 'The God of your fathers has sent me to you, 'and they say to me, 'What is His name? 'what shall I say to them?" (Exodus 3:13 [NKJV]).

He didn't say, "Tell them 'I *was* 'sent to you." He didn't say, "Tell them 'I *will be* sent you." No. The past is the past, and tomorrow isn't promised to us. God's response was to tell them "I AM has sent me to you" (Exodus 3:14 [NKJV]).

God is the "Great I AM." He is the present God of "right now!" Now is the time for the Church to awaken and rise up!

BIBLIOGRAPHY

Assembly Bill A416. New York S. (2021).

  https://www.nysenate.gov/legislation/bills/2021/a416.

Blue Letter Bible, s.v. "Dictionary and Word Search for *krateo*

  (Strong's 2902)." Accessed February 12, 2021.

  https://www.blbclassic.org/lang/lexicon/lexicon.cfm?S
  trongs=G2902&t=KJV.

California Code Register Section 1861(b). (2020).

  https://casetext.com/regulation/california-code-of-
  regulations/title-13-motor-vehicles/division-2-
  department-of-the-california-highway-patrol/chapter-
  11-rules-applicable-to-use-of-state-property/article-3-

restrictions-on-use-of-state-buildings-and-

grounds/section-1861-prohibited-conduct

California Health and Safety Code Resister Section 120275.

(1996).

Campbell, Josh. "These 'high risk 'California sex offenders

were released early. A prosecutor warns they're still a

threat." CNN Wire Service. May 8, 2020.

https://www.mercurynews.com/2020/05/08/these-

high-risk-california-sex-offenders-were-released-

early-a-prosecutor-warns-theyre-still-a-threat/.

"COVID-19 INDUSTRY GUIDANCE: Places of Worship and

Providers of Religious Services and Cultural

Ceremonies." California Department of Public Health.

July 29, 2020.

https://files.covid19.ca.gov/pdf/guidance-places-of-

worship--en.pdf.

Equal Restroom Access Act. Assembly Bill No. 1732.

California S. Chapter 818. (2016).

https://leginfo.legislature.ca.gov/faces/billTextClient.x

html?bill_id=201520160AB1732.

Exemption from tax on corporations, certain trusts, etc. 26
    U.S.C. § 501(c)(3) (1954).
    https://uscode.house.gov/view.xhtml?req=(title:26%20
    section:501%20edition:prelim)%20OR%20(granuleid:
    USC-prelim-title26-
    section501)&f=treesort&num=0&edition=prelim.

"Flat Earth International Conference (USA) 2019." Flat Earth
    International Conference. http://fe2019.com/.

Hodges, Mark. "Nancy Pelosi: Gay 'marriage 'is 'consistent '
    with Catholic teaching." LifeSiteNews. Accessed June
    2, 2015. https://www.lifesitenews.com/news/nancy-
    pelosi-gay-marriage-is-consistent-with-catholic-
    teaching.

Holcombe, Madeline, and Eric Levenson. "Covid-19 vaccine
    en route to every state as health officials say they
    hope immunizations begin Monday." *CNN*.
    December 13, 2020.
    https://www.cnn.com/2020/12/13/health/us-
    coronavirus-sunday/index.html.

Hurley, Lawrence. "U.S. Supreme Court backs Christian

    baker who rebuffed gay couple." The Washington

    Post. June 4, 2020. https://www.reuters.com/article/us-

    usa-court-baker/u-s-supreme-court-backs-christian-

    baker-who-rebuffed-gay-couple-idUSK

Longley, Robert. "What Is Incrementalism in Government?

    Definition and Examples." ThoughtCo. October 14,

    2020. https://www.thoughtco.com/what-is-

    incrementalism-in-government-5082043.

MacDonald, Andrew, and Ed Stetzer. "The Lasting Legacy of

    the Jesus People: How an Unlikely, Countercultural

    Movement went Mainstream," *Talbot*

    Magazine (blog), Biola University, July 17, 2020,

    https://www.biola.edu/blogs/talbot-

    magazine/2020/the-lasting-legacy-of-the-jesus-people.

Medved, Michael. "What's the Truth About the First

    Thanksgiving." Posted November 13, 2017. PragerU.

    5:43. https://www.prageru.com/video/whats-the-

    truth-about-the-first-thanksgiving/.

"Nero Persecutes the Christians, 64 A.D." EyeWitness to

History. 2000.

http://www.eyewitnesstohistory.com/christians.htm.

News Staff, "Riverside county launches mobile app to report

nonessential businesses." NBC Palm Springs. April

10, 2020.

https://nbcpalmsprings.com/2020/04/10/riverside-

county-launches-mobile-app-to-report-nonessential-

businesses/

"NO OPT-OUT ALLOWED: The California Sex Ed

Indoctrination," June 26, 2019. Uploaded by Jeremiah

Films. Vimeo. 31:32. https://vimeo.com/344632997.

Senate Bill 145. New York S. (2019).

https://www.nysenate.gov/legislation/bills/2021/a416.

Singleton, Marilyn M. America's Frontline Doctors, M.D.

https://www.americasfrontlinedoctors.com/wp-

content/uploads/2020/09/Masks-Science.pdf.

"Spying on Family and Friends." *Holocaust and Human

Behavior.* Facing History and Ourselves. Accessed

February 12, 2021.
https://www.facinghistory.org/holocaust-and-human-behavior/chapter-6/spying-family-and-friends.

"Teen Health Resources & Information." TeenSource.
Accessed February 12, 2021.
https://www.teensource.org/.

Turban, Jack. "What Is Gender Dysphoria?" American
Psychiatric Association. November 2020.
https://www.psychiatry.org/patients-families/gender-dysphoria/what-is-gender-dysphoria.

Wallsten, Kevin, and Rachel VanSickle-Ward. "What's next
after the Supreme Court's birth control ruling?" The
Washington Post. July 18, 2020.
https://www.washingtonpost.com/politics/2020/07/18/
whats-next-after-supreme-courts-birth-control-ruling/

Williams, Christina Barnes. "The Jesus People Movement
and the Awakening of the Late 1960s." (master's
thesis, College of William & Mary, 2002).
https://dx.doi.org/doi:10.21220/s2-ss4e-cs11.

Ziemer, Heidi. "The Burned-Over District." *Two Hundred Years on the Erie Canal.* New York Heritage Digital Collections, September 20, 2019. https://nyheritage.org/exhibits/

ABOUT THE AUTHOR

Tim Thompson is the founding pastor of 412 Church Murrieta. He also founded Our Watch with Tim Thompson, a Christian non-profit organization that envisions a future where the conservative voice becomes the dominating force in California politics and seeks to be a conduit to provide ways to activate and unite conservatives throughout the state, standing firm for parental rights. He is a loving husband and father of two. He and his wife Nicky have been married since 1996.

He is a preacher/teacher of eschatology, and a leader in engaging the Church in the political arena by dealing with sensitive issues to have a positive impact on our culture.

Pastor Tim has a strong desire to WIN people for Jesus (Acts 4:12), help them in their growth as a DISCIPLE of Jesus (Hebrews 4:12), and SEND them out to continue the work of the Gospel (Ephesians 4:12). That mission focus is well evident in all aspects of his ministry.

Made in USA - Kendallville, IN
98752_9798714572890
10.25.2024 2051